"As a good teacher, Hexham is not afraid to offer the kind of opinion or insight that is bound to provoke discussion and debate. This book is the fruit of many years of trying to encourage university students to engage meaningfully with the study of religion."

Gerald J. Pillay, vice-chancellor and rector,
Liverpool Hope University

"Hexham offers an introduction to the study of religions based on his years of teaching the subject, an impressive multicultural knowledge of various religious traditions."

Larry Hurtado, emeritus professor of New
Testament language, literature and theology,
University of Edinburgh

"Hexham is well known to his many readers through his publications on religious studies, both as a general field of research, as well as represented in various movements, both local and worldwide."

Gary R. Habermas, distinguished research professor
and chair of the department of philosophy
and theology, Liberty University

"Hexham's book is a resource that brings clarity to the vast world of religious beliefs. This needs to be on the bookshelf of every Christian leader."

Rev. Dr. Carson Pue, Trinity Western University

ENCOUNTERING
WORLD
RELIGIONS

A Christian Introduction

ENCOUNTERING
WORLD
RELIGIONS

irving
HEXHAM

ZONDERVAN
ACADEMIC

ZONDERVAN ACADEMIC

Encountering World Religions
Copyright © 2019 by Irving Hexham

ISBN 978-0-310-58860-3 (softcover)

ISBN 978-0-310-58861-0 (ebook)

Requests for information should be addressed to:
Zondervan, *3900 Sparks Dr. SE, Grand Rapids, Michigan 49546*

Cover image: Moustache Girl/Shutterstock
Interior design: Kait Lamphere

Printed in the United States of America

19 20 21 22 23 24 25 26 27 28 29 /LSC/ 15 14 13 12 11 10 9 8 7 6 5 4 3 2 1

To my wife, Karla Poewe

Contents

Acknowledgments

Having acknowledged my academic mentors in my earlier book *Understanding World Religions*, this is the place to recognize all those who encouraged me following my evangelical conversion at the age of eighteen. This led to an enormous change in my life from being an apprentice gas fitter in Stockport, England, to eventually becoming a professor of Religious Studies in Canada.

Among the many people who helped me as a young Christian are Peter and Judy Heyman, Jillian and Jeremy Jackson, Peter Downham, Peter and Dorothy Wilkinson, Colin Buchanan, Trevor and Liz Watts, Richard Bibby, Paula Nicholson, and Clark Pinnock, who suggested that I visit the Swiss L'Abri. There I met Francis Schaeffer, who was the first person to encourage me to go to university. L'Abri workers Ranald and Sue Macaulay and Joe and Linette Martin were also helpful and encouraging. Ward and Laurel Gasque were enormously helpful and responsible for my moving to Canada to work at Regent College.

Others who need to be thanked are Roger and Sue Mitchell, David Virtue, Larry Hurtado, Bruce Waltke, Richard Pierard, John Warwick Montgomery, Carl Armerding, Tim Callaway, David Bosch, Michael Cassidy, Frank and Rosemary Eyck, and my doctoral supervisors Kenneth Ingham and Fred Welbourn, all of whom shaped my understanding of both academia and Christianity. I must also thank Tim Callaway, Chang-Han Kim, Greg Purdy, Ron Galloway, Doug Barrie, and my son Jeremy for their comments on this work. Finally, I'm grateful to my colleagues Tony Barber and Elisabeth Rohlman, as well as a host of students from numerous religious traditions who took my courses at the University of Calgary. They inspired me and corrected my misunderstandings of their own religious traditions.

Preface

This book is written for Christians living at a time when they increasingly encounter people belonging to other religious traditions as neighbors, colleagues, coworkers, and fellow students. Its aim is to help Christians who have little understanding of the major world religions to be able to better communicate with others.

The book does not offer easy answers or an ABC of how to convert someone who belongs to another religious tradition. Rather, it seeks to help Christians recognize that accepting the truth of the gospel often takes many years when a person has grown up as a Buddhist, Hindu, Jew, or Muslim. Understanding should precede criticism, and friendship is the basis for living together in a shared society.

As Christians we believe that all truth is God's truth and that everyone is created in God's image. We are commanded to spread the gospel, but we need to remember that personal evangelism rests on the establishment of trust. We need to take a real interest in our friends and acquaintances and learn to understand what they believe and why.

This approach may seem not direct enough, too wishy-washy for some, but the examples of the New Testament, church history, and, often, personal experience show that people turn to Christ when they see his truth reflected in the lives of believers. It is my hope that this book will encourage you in your Christian witness while also strengthening your faith in the knowledge that Christianity is true, and that we have nothing to fear from exposure to the beliefs of others.

chapter one

Welcome Back to the First Century

Introduction

After almost fifteen hundred years of Christian civilization in the West, we now live in a world where many people are deliberately turning their backs on the Christian tradition. At the same time, believers of other major world religions are establishing themselves in what were formerly "Christian" countries.

Not all who lived in so-called Christian countries in the past were devoted Christians, but Christianity shaped people's lives and provided the framework for society as a whole in terms of ethics and shared beliefs. Today this framework is shattered, and we face a situation that Western Christians have not encountered for at least a thousand years. In fact, in many ways, our society is returning to a situation remarkably similar to the beginning of the Christian era when the gospel was first proclaimed throughout what was then the Roman world.

Therefore, it is worth spending time thinking about how early Christian missionaries, and those who later converted northern and eastern Europe to Christianity, presented their faith and what it tells us about our own time.

Paul in Athens

The story of the apostle Paul preaching in Athens about "an unknown God" is well known to most Christians, but it can be easy to overlook its significance for the present time (Acts 17:16–34). Let us consider for a moment ancient Athens in the first century AD. The great British biblical commentator William Barkley reminds us that "Athens had long since left behind her great days of action but she was still the greatest university town in the world, to which men seeking learning came from all over. She was a city of many gods. It was said that there were more statues of the gods in Athens than in all the rest of Greece put together and that in Athens it was easier to meet a god than a man."[1]

Among the educated classes that encountered Paul, there were two main groups. There were the Epicureans, who believed that everything was a matter of chance, life ended at death, and the gods were not interested in humans. The only thing to do was enjoy life. The other group were the Stoics, who held to a form of pantheism, believing that God's spirit penetrated everything and gave humans life. As a result, people lived as long as they did because a spark of God animated their bodies. In this view everything was determined by God and must be accepted as the hand of fate. Consequently, all life was part of an eternal cycle that flourished and then crashed in a great cataclysm only to begin again in an endless cycle of creation and destruction.

What is important is that when St. Paul encountered the intellectuals of Athens, he adapted his preaching to allow himself to speak into their world of thought and action. Because he was so successful in doing this, many liberal biblical critics have questioned whether the speech recorded in Acts could possibly be authentic to Paul.

Commenting on these doubts, New Testament scholar F. F. Bruce, a classical scholar before he turned to study of the Bible, pointed out that, generally speaking, only theologians have a problem with Paul's speech at Athens. The majority of classical scholars who specialize in the study of ancient Greece have no problem accepting the speech as authentic and argue that it has all the marks of authenticity. In support of his argument, Bruce compared Paul's speeches in Antioch and Lystra, noting that Paul often adapted his message to his audience.[2]

It is not surprising that when Paul was in Athens, he did not quote the Hebrew Bible, which would have been unfamiliar to most of his hearers. Rather, he cited Greek poets. Nor did he engage in a philosophical argument with appeals to biblical revelation. Instead, he started his argument by noting that the Athenians were remarkably religious. Then he demonstrated that he was a careful observer of his surroundings and Athenian society by mentioning that he had seen an altar dedicated "to an unknown God" (Acts 17:23).

After making this observation, he proclaimed the true nature of God, concluding his declaration with a quotation from a poem attributed to the Cretan philosopher Epimenides (sixth century BC). He followed this with a quotation from the Greek *Phainomena* by Cilician writer Aratus (315–240 BC). By using these verses, Paul demonstrated to his hearers that he was an educated man well versed in Greek literature and thought. Only then did he go on to proclaim the gospel in no uncertain terms. As a result, some people made fun of him, others said they would like to know more, and a few spent time with him and became believers.

Commenting on this passage in the eighth century AD, the early English Christian writer known as "the father of English history," the Venerable Bede (672–735), wrote, "The apostle's argument deserves careful examination."[3] He then showed his readers how Paul carefully crafted his message to his hearers and did not appeal to biblical writers they did not know. Rather, he addressed them on the basis of "the testimony of their own authors."[4] Bede concluded, "Surely it is the mark of great knowledge to . . . take into account the particular individuals who are one's listeners."[5]

Bede observed that the writer of Acts noted that one of the

converts was Dionysius, a prominent citizen who, according to tradition, went on to become the Bishop of Corinth and, in some accounts, the Bishop of Athens itself. F. F. Bruce pointed out that the mention of women listening to Paul's preaching means they must have been educated. What this account of Paul's preaching does is lay down a pattern for evangelism and mission in societies where there is little or no knowledge of the Bible.[6]

Paul's Advice about Living in a Non-Christian World

Paul, in his letters, frequently addressed real problems facing Christian communities scattered across the Roman world. Among these problems was the question of how Christians should treat food in societies where, before it was sold and during preparation, it was often presented to various gods and laid out before idols to gain a spiritual blessing.

Paul's responses to such questions were always based on Scripture and the realities of the situation people were facing. In the case of "food offered to idols," he begins by pointing out that idols are images made by humans, and the gods they represent have no real existence. The food is perfectly edible. The problem is not the food or the fact that someone performed a religious act intended to add spiritual power to it. The problem was that some new converts, weak in faith, might misunderstand and think they were participating in a pagan rite. In 1 Corinthians 8:1–13, Paul tells his readers that for the sake of the weaker Christian, one should not give the impression that one had participated in such a ritual.

He advises Christians to avoid pagan feasts and public displays of devotion to pagan gods. But if a non-Christian friend invites a Christian to dinner, the Christian can decide what to do and does not need to ask if the food was sacrificed to idols before eating it. The key issue for Paul, as he makes clear in 1 Corinthians 10, is one of conscience and not endangering the faith of a younger Christian. As he writes in 1 Corinthians 10:23, "'I have the right to do anything'— but not everything is constructive."

This principle means that Christians are to make an informed judgment and act in a way that honors God by presenting a clear witness to others. Paul concludes his discussion of food sacrificed to idols in 1 Corinthians 10:31–33 by saying, "So whether you eat or drink or whatever you do, do it all for the glory of God. Do not cause anyone to stumble, whether Jews, Greeks or the church of God— even as I try to please everyone in every way. For I am not seeking my own good but the good of many, so that they may be saved."

These verses are well known to most Christians and used frequently as a guideline for behavior, particularly regarding how one interacts with non-believers. What is often overlooked is that for at least the last fifteen hundred years, the "non-believer" in Western societies was someone just like oneself who simply did not believe in God or live in a Christian manner. Now the situation has changed, and we in the West are once more living in a society that is far closer to Paul's time than any society since at least the early Middle Ages. Today many people we meet are no longer non-believers who reject their Christian heritage; they are true believers in other religions. When we seek to apply passages from 1 Corinthians, we must realize our social context has changed.

Take a close look at these passages and similar ones in the New Testament. Notice that it is taken for granted that Christians live alongside members of other religions described as "pagan." What is particularly interesting is that it is assumed Christians would be on good terms with these people and might be invited to their homes for a meal.

This raises a question: "How many non-Christians do you or I know with whom we are on close enough terms to visit their homes and eat meals with them?" Perhaps not many. Yet Paul assumes friendship is the basis of at least one form of evangelism, and he roots this belief firmly in his biblical understanding of God as the creator of all people, as he points out in 1 Corinthians 8:4–6.

Evangelism in a Post-Christian Society: A Personal Approach

In July 2011, Mark Howell, pastor of communities at Canyon Ridge Christian Church in Las Vegas, Nevada, wrote in his blog: "Honestly, if you would've told me 25 years ago that I'd need a resource that would help me understand world religions, I'd probably rolled my eyes and said, 'I have no plans to be a missionary.' . . . In 2011 we live in a very different culture, post-Christian America, and developing an understanding of other religions is essential." He then went on to recommend my earlier book *Understanding World Religions*[7] as a way "to get up to speed on the beliefs and, more importantly, on the worldview of representatives of the other major religions."[8]

Since then I've come to realize that Mark had two advantages that many may lack. First, he was theologically educated and able to apply what he read in the book. Second, he admits that growing up in Southern California, he knew Buddhists and Muslims as friends and was prepared for living in a religiously plural society.

Unfortunately, many of us are not as fortunate as Mark in knowing how to approach members of other religious traditions. This book was written to introduce Christians to other religious traditions and to help us relate our beliefs to people who embrace religions very different from our own. But before we begin talking about specific world religions, it is important for Christians to reflect on the Bible and how they can live their faith in a rapidly changing multi-religious society.

The Biblical Framework

The Bible begins by proclaiming the great truth that God created the heavens and the earth. It continues by telling the story of the creation of humankind and states very clearly that all people are made in the image of God. Not surprisingly, given the fact that God is the creator of all things, we are told in Genesis 1 that he surveyed his creation and saw that it was good.

Today many people laugh at the biblical story and see it as a relic from a pre-scientific age. "Don't Christians realize," they say, "that we now know life was created by a process of evolution. Bible stories are fables without any relevance to the modern world." Although this is a popular view, it is wrong. It overlooks the uniqueness of the biblical account of creation and what it really teaches about the world and our place in it.

What most secular people, and even some Christians, do not realize is just how revolutionary the story of Genesis is. To begin with, it tells us that the world God created was and is good. This may not seem very profound, but it is. It contradicts many views in popular philosophies and religions. For example, ancient traditions found in Greek and Roman philosophy saw the world as essentially bad. Buddhism and the Hindu tradition both see the world as an illusion that we need to escape. In one way or another, these and other religions teach that the earth and the material things we see around us are essentially bad and something humans need to overcome and escape from.

Plato (428–347 BC) understood the true essence of the human being in terms of an immortal soul trapped in a material body. This the Bible clearly denies. The Bible is world affirming and teaches that material things are good, not bad, and are there to be enjoyed by humans.

The Bible teaches that God created the human race, which means everyone you know and have ever met, in his own image. Thus, all human beings share the ability to establish a relationship with God and with each other. The Bible teaches us that however different people look, or seem, they share a common humanity. Once again, this teaching stands in sharp contrast with many views that are popular today.

What makes people who they are at the most fundamental level is not their ancestors or a specific culture, but the fact that they are created by God and share his image. Of course, we must not be naive and think that our background, parents, culture, and ancestry have no impact on us. Each of our personal histories is important and shapes our outlook and our lives. But whatever our histories, they can never diminish God's image in us and in everyone we meet.

A corollary of the belief that God created humans in his image is rejection of the idea that the human races evolved from different ancestors and are therefore essentially different. Christians stood firmly against what in the late nineteenth and early twentieth centuries was known as "scientific racism"[9] and should continue that stand today. In the biblical perspective, there are no human races; there is only one human race that developed from common ancestors. The story of Adam and Eve, quaint as it may sound to modern ears, commits Christians to reject racism and everything derived from it.

What does all of this have to do with world religions and the increasingly religiously plural society most of us live in today? The first chapters of Genesis not only lay the foundation for all that follows in the Bible but also provide a context for our understanding of world religions. They portray a world in which humanity began in relationship with God and has an understanding of him. In Romans 1:19–23, Paul writes that humans continue to have a sense of God, and creation itself witnesses to his existence.

The Bible leads us to expect that humans would seek God and, as a result of the fall, that such seeking would lead to false religious traditions alongside worship of the true God. While the Bible clearly condemns misplaced worship, it doesn't disparage humans' need for God or their innate, if sometimes suppressed, knowledge of him.[10]

This inner longing of all people for God was well expressed by the great Christian leader St. Augustine of Hippo (354–430 AD) in his *Confessions*. He wrestled with people's attempt to worship God without knowing him, or at least without having revealed knowledge of him. He concluded that the rise of non-Christian religions was due to the naturalness of the human search for God and the fact that to know the true God one needs instruction. This is the evangelistic task before us. The big question is how do we go about it?

People Matter More Than Ideas or Things

Christians are familiar with the story of the Good Samaritan found in Luke 10:25–37, and preachers often cite it as an example of how we should treat others. Samaritans were the equivalent of modern-day Jehovah's Witnesses, Mormons, or Muslims. They shared some aspects of Jewish beliefs and practice. They even claimed that they worshiped the same God. But Jews saw them as heretical cultists and wanted nothing to do with them because they watered down Jewish laws and practices.

This story can speak to our situation of relating to non-Christians. In the parable, Jesus recognized and praised the Samaritan's good deeds, but he did not take the next step of saying what the Samaritan believed was true about God or an alternate path to God. What Jesus shows us is that it is possible to recognize the good in someone of another faith without agreeing with all of their beliefs.

A similar situation occurred when Jesus encountered a Roman centurion in Matthew 8:5–13. When the centurion asks Jesus to heal his servant, Jesus praises him: "Truly I tell you, I have not found anyone in Israel with such great faith." Some interpret this passage to indicate that the centurion was not a Jew but was on the way to converting to Judaism. Yet the passage gives no such indication. As a Roman centurion the man, as part of his duties, would have regularly offered sacrifices to Roman gods and vowed allegiance to Caesar, who was recognized as a god. What does this tell us?

The consistent message we get from Jesus is that we must meet people where they are. This does not include approving their beliefs or arguing, like Bishop Spong[11] and Gretta Vosper,[12] that we must abandon Christian orthodoxy to embrace a "new situation." Jesus said nothing like that. Instead he recognized that people are complex and, unlike him, we do not see their hearts or know their inner thoughts.

Whether people are Buddhists, Christians, Hindus, Jews, Muslims, or followers of another religious belief system or none, they are all made in the image of God and have a personal history we rarely know. Our duty is to befriend them, help them understand the gospel, and invite them to accept Jesus as their Savior. God alone sees their hearts; we must be careful how we respond and not condemn.

To respect them as God's image-bearers, we need to make an effort to understand them, what they believe and why, and the way they live. That is part of seeking to see them with the eyes of Christ and to reach out to them wherever they are.

Unfortunately, today we live in an age of instant results, and this can cause us as Christians to see conversion in a similar manner. Sudden conversions are biblical and possible, as we see in the experience of the apostle Paul, St. Augustine, John Wesley, Billy Graham, and many other Christians through the ages. Many people experience slow conversions that take place over many years. This was something I learned from Francis Schaeffer at the Swiss L'Abri. At first, I was shocked by the lax attitude L'Abri had in encouraging people to make a confession of faith. When I asked Schaeffer about this, he said something to the effect of, "Wait and see. If you stay in touch with us for long enough, you will learn that God is in charge and many people become Christians after long years of slowly struggling to understand."

Experience has taught me the wisdom of his words. Far too often, sudden conversions can make a big splash but ultimately lead nowhere, while those who take years to become Christians turn out to be the most solid converts. This was the case with C. S. Lewis, who was, and remains, one of the most influential Christians of modern times.

A Brief History of Changing Religious Attitudes in the West

Before beginning our survey of world religions, it will be helpful to briefly sketch Christianity's decline in the West. What moved Europe and North America from their Christian heritage to the pluralistic, secular, and sometimes hostile views toward Christianity we now see? Within living memory, Christianity was respected by most Westerners regardless of whether they were Christians. Christianity was recognized as the basis of Western law, the arts, social behavior, and most of what was considered good in society.

Today Christianity is no longer looked up to as the foundation of Western civilization. The reason is rarely taught in public schools in anything like a systematic manner. Yet an understanding of history and the way our society changed from one grounded in the Christian tradition to today's increasingly anti-Christian perspective is essential to anyone hoping to present the gospel to their neighbors.

To put modern unbelief in context, one must realize that Christianity emerged in a Roman Empire that was technologically more advanced than anything that followed it until the late eighteenth and early nineteenth centuries. As a result, educated people in Western Europe and the European societies of early North America, at least until the middle of the eighteenth century, were aware that their technology and knowledge were generally inferior to those of the Romans. The classical world of Greece and Rome was viewed as worthy of emulation and provided a vision of the future through recapturing the glories of the past.

This respect for the ancient world carried with it a corresponding respect for Christianity. Textbooks used in schools and universities referred back to Greek, Roman, and Christian authors as the basis of civilization, and because the Greeks and Romans had converted to Christianity, it was understood that Christianity was valuable and true.

In a fifty-year period from 1775 to 1825, everything changed. The discipline of "natural philosophy," which later became known as "science," developed in new directions, and things the Romans had never achieved became possible. Gradually, the Romans came to be seen as just another ancient and unscientific people.

This led to new critiques of Christianity by writers like Edward Gibbon (1737–1794), who saw history as the record of human folly. He argued that the Romans were well on the way to creating the modern world, developing things like steam engines and modern technology, until they embraced Christianity. It was Christianity that led them astray, causing them to lose their ability to think in terms of what was gradually becoming recognized as science. With books like Gibbon's *History of the Decline and Fall of the Roman Empire* (1776–1789), Christians were put on the defensive. The ancient worlds of Greece and Rome came to be seen as a great project that had failed because of Christianity.

The arguments of Gibbon and those who followed him were flawed. Numerous factors led to the collapse of the Western Roman Empire. In the eastern Mediterranean, the other half of the empire continued as Byzantium for another thousand years. Yet popular perception had been changed.

Once the conversion of the Roman Empire to Christianity was questioned and presented as a disaster that prevented the development of science, arguments of skeptics became easier to accept. Christianity, which had grown under the protection of Roman achievements, came to be seen as the cause of centuries of economic and intellectual stagnation. This outlook was expressed, for example, in the labeling of the medieval era as the "Dark Ages." Blaming Christianity for opposing science was unwarranted; the sixteenth- and seventeenth-century scientific revolution was led by Christians. But a persuasive propaganda had arisen for people who wanted to abandon Christianity.

Perhaps equally important for the West in the long term was

a little-known religious revolution that occurred in India, where a carefully coordinated attack on Christian missions had a devastating impact. It also led to the evangelization of the West by Buddhists and Hindus.

As early as the 1840s, Muslim scholars in India, to undermine the Bible and defend Islam, were citing German biblical critics. By the 1850s, such attacks on Christian preaching became a tidal wave, sweeping through India and other Muslim countries.

In India, the works of biblical critics such as J. D. Michaelis (1717–1791), J. C. Eichhorn (1752–1827), and D. F. Strauss (1808–1874) were standard works cited by Muslims to prove the unreliability of the Bible. They also referred to the works of various other writers whose work gave birth to the anti-Christian rationalist creed of deism, such as John Toland (1670–1722), Thomas Chubb (1679–1747), Baruch Spinoza (1632–1677), Herman Reimarus (1694–1768), Voltaire (1694–1778), and Rousseau (1712–1778).[13]

Later in the nineteenth century this concerted attack changed from an attempt to merely blunt the impact of Christian evangelism in India and other parts of Asia to the development of a mission strategy to promote Buddhism, Hinduism, and, to a lesser extent, Islam in the West. This new strategy was adopted by members of the Theosophical Society founded in New York in November 1875 by lapsed Christians turned Spiritualists. Two of its founders, Helena Petrovna Blavatsky (1831–1891) and Colonel Henry Steel Olcott (1832–1907), moved to India in 1879, where they began their work of counter-evangelism in cooperation with the Hindu revivalist movement Arya Samaj. Later their crusade was taken up by their English disciple, the former agnostic Annie Besant (1847–1933), who converted to Theosophy in 1889.

Olcott in particular rallied non-Christian religious leaders against what he called "the Christian enemy." In a letter to a Buddhist monk in Sri Lanka, the Venerable Piyaratana Tissa, dated August 29, 1878, Olcott wrote, "The Western world is dying of brutal sensuality and ignorance; come and help rescue it." He went on to say that the Theosophical Society was founded as a brotherhood of humanity and "league of religions against the common enemy—Christianity."[14]

As a result of these efforts, Indian religions were exported to the West, often taught by charismatic leaders like Hindu Swami Vivekananda (1863–1902) and Buddhist Daisetsu Teitaro (D. T.) Suzuki (1870–1966), both of whom were influenced by Theosophy. In the West, aspects of the Hindu tradition and Buddhism, though not Islam, came to be seen as an alternative to "the stifling moralism and anti-scientific ethos of Christianity."[15]

The importance of these developments should not be underestimated. They caused Eastern religions to be seen positively by many living in America and Europe, while Christianity was seen as a disaster. It is in this context that we as Christians now seek to share Christ with followers of other world religions.

chapter two

The Experiential Core of Primal Religions

Introduction

Traditional religions that lack scriptures are practiced by millions of people worldwide. These religions were aptly called "primal religions" by Anglican missionary John V. Turner (1914–2001). What he meant by the term "primal religions" is a spirituality and longing for the divine similar to that experienced by St. Augustine of Hippo before he became a Christian.[1]

To help people understand the way primal experiences shape religion, we will use African traditional religions and their interaction with Christianity as an example. It may seem strange to write about "primal" or "traditional" religions by talking about them in the context of Christianity. This is necessary because what in the past were distinct religious traditions in traditional societies are today interwoven with world religions as a result of worldwide modernization. Consequently, practically no "pure" traditional religions exist because even very remote areas of the world are impacted by the West through radio, television, and the internet.

A recent Pew Research survey provides the context for Africa. Today 62.9 percent of Africans identify as Christians, 30.2 percent identify as Muslims, and only 3.3 percent claim to be members of traditional religions.[2] Other research shows that when Africans identify with traditional religions, the vast majority incorporate elements of Christianity or Islam, depending on where they live.

As a result, primal experiences in societies where the majority of people converted to Christianity within the last 150 years are often blended experiences. For example, Joshua, a well-educated teacher and member of a Presbyterian church living in Johannesburg, told the following story.

Shortly after his father's death, while Joshua was preparing to go to the funeral near Durban, his dead father appeared to him in a dream to tell him that he must take a train and not drive to Durban. When he told his younger brother and two cousins, they were skeptical and insisted that he was simply "stressed out."

That evening, they drove while he went by train, which was more expensive. When he arrived in Durban, relatives told him that his brother and two cousins were killed in a car accident on the road from Pietermaritzburg to Durban. Shocked by this incident, he saw a psychiatrist. When that did not help, he found a traditional diviner, who cured him of his anxiety attacks. Later, he became a part-time assistant to his diviner. He stopped attending the Presbyterian church, which did not approve of such things, and began attending a small African independent church, which welcomed his "spiritual gifts."

To talk meaningfully about primal experiences in contemporary society, it is necessary to see these experiences in terms of this type of complex interaction. Today traditional religions that lack their own scriptures are united by the universality of primal experiences and their willingness to incorporate aspects, and sometimes the scriptures, of world religions.[3]

Explaining the Inexplicable

To understand African and other traditional religions that lack scriptures, we must enter as fully as possible into the perspective of someone living in a traditional society where inexplicable phenomena are often seen as an expression of mysterious powers. It is easy to dismiss beliefs of this type and see them as unscientific. Yet we need to begin by recognizing how common reports of strange experiences are throughout the world, including in the post-Enlightenment and post-industrial societies of today.

Primal experiences are unexpected, vivid encounters that are abnormal and give rise to religious beliefs and practices. One way of viewing primal experiences is to see them as "threshold experiences" that bring people to a crisis in their lives. It is important to note that when a primal experience occurs, both in the West and in other parts of the world where reporting such experiences is more common, the initial reaction is often one of shock and bewilderment.

This type of reaction occurs throughout the world where secular forms of Western education have taken root. Surprisingly, such reactions are also reported in traditional African, Buddhist, Hindu, and Islamic societies where people are taught to expect supernatural events yet still are deeply shocked when they encounter them. When the shock wears off, either they react in a way that changes their lives, such as joining a religious group or changing from a nominal believer to a deeply committed one, or they mentally shelve the experience they remember as remarkable but which does not affect the way they live or think.

In his groundbreaking book *Visions of Jesus*,[4] Canadian professor Phillip H. Wiebe documents the fact that in North America, visions of Jesus are far more common than most people realize, and people from all walks of life claim to have met Jesus. These experiences occur in dreams, in apparitions occurring in broad daylight, and in cases where people describe themselves as "half-awake." What they have in common is that the people immediately recognized Jesus and have no doubt about who they encountered. Many claim Jesus spoke to them and identified himself before giving them a message. Others simply saw him. Stories like those Wiebe collected are also common in Africa and other parts of the world, although in India people are more likely to encounter Krishna rather than Jesus.

Wiebe was surprised that a significant minority of his informants said the experience was very moving and something they will never forget, but otherwise made no difference in their life. This was in sharp contrast to the majority who told him that their encounter with Jesus changed their life, and they became convinced Christians.

Africans in South Africa reported similar reactions when we interviewed people at a large charismatic church in Durban. Some told us how they had encountered Jesus or met an ancestor who pointed them to Christ. We also were told about friends and relatives of the interviewee who were not Christians who had had similar experiences. The people involved turned to traditional African religions or, in one case, became a Muslim.

These eyewitness accounts of visions of Jesus are remarkably similar to other visions and strange experiences that occur in different religious and secular contexts. Africans meet their ancestors, Buddhists see visions of the Buddha, Hindus claim to encounter gods like Krishna, Jews are visited by relatives who died in the Holocaust, and Muslims have experiences involving great Muslim saints. In Western society, people claim to see UFOs and meet aliens from outer space.

In most cases, the primal experiences people report reflect the culture in which they live and, usually, their own religious background. There are, of course, exceptions, such as Sadhu Sundar Singh (1889–1929) who told how, as a young man practicing Sikh, he met Jesus. This event changed his life, and he became a very effective Christian missionary.[5]

There are reports of other types of encounters with God that are neither Christian nor pagan, but which prepare the way for individuals and groups to become Christians. A good example is the South African Xhosa prophet Ntsikana. After a series of profound primal experiences that took place within the context of Xhosa traditional religion, he composed what became known as his "Great Hymn" to the glory of the one true God who promised to send his messengers to the Xhosa. This hymn, and Ntsikana's preaching, caused him and thousands of Xhosa to embrace Christianity once missionaries arrived in the area.[6]

The forms that primal experiences take vary according to the predominant social and cultural context. They normally are life changing, although in a small number of cases they make no difference in a person's life. They are simply considered inexplicable. As we saw with Wiebe's interviewees, this is also true of encounters with Christ.

When someone says their life was changed by such an experience, it becomes a threshold experience that opens the door to a new way of life. What all of this shows, as St. Augustine observed, is that we are all created with an innate longing for God that may take us, as it did Augustine, in many wrong directions before we finally come to know the true God as revealed in the Bible.

Another Type of Vision

Before becoming an academic, I served a six-year gas-fitting apprenticeship in Stockport, England, with the British North Western Gas Board. At that time the University of Manchester was expanding, and many people who lived nearby were turning their large old Victorian houses into apartments to rent to students. The gas fitter I served most of my apprenticeship with was Fred, a former paratrooper who had served in an elite British regiment and often talked about his military experiences. He had a friend called Paddy, who had served in the elite British regiment Coldstream Guards. Both men seemed fearless.[7]

One Monday morning I turned up at work to find that neither Fred nor Paddy had any tools with them, which was unthinkable. They explained that they had left them the previous night at a house where they were installing new bathrooms to create student apartments. So another apprentice and I drove with them to a house near the university where they were working. They let themselves in, and we saw that their tools were scattered all over the place. They told us to hurry up. We collected their tools and left as quickly as possible. We then went for breakfast where we met another group of gas fitters and their apprentices. In the safety of the café, they told us what had happened.

About nine o'clock the previous evening, they turned off their blowlamps and were ready to pack their tools. It was pitch-black outside. A young woman appeared, coming down the stairs from the attic area above where they were working. They were astonished because the front door was locked, and they had been the only people in the house all day. They asked who she was and how she got in without them seeing her. The woman ignored them and sat down on a stair about halfway down the stairs. She looked distressed and was crying. Then she placed her head in her hands and vanished.

Both men were shocked. They grabbed their jackets, made sure everything was safe, and ran out of the house as fast as possible. Once outside, and this was years before cell phones, they found a phone booth and telephoned the owner of the house. Still shaken, they told him what had happened. He was not surprised. He told them that two years before, a young woman who was renting a room in the attic had committed suicide on the stairs.

Both Fred and Paddy were convinced that they had seen a ghost and admitted that it really scared them. They refused to continue working on the job even though they lost a lot of money for not completing their contract. What surprised me and the others present was that these two battle-hardened soldiers admitted they were scared by what they had experienced in that old house in Manchester. They never mentioned it again, always refusing to talk about what they had seen whenever we tried to get them to talk about it. Something very unusual had happened that night.

I have no doubt that Fred and Paddy were telling the truth. I have never seen anyone else so visibly in shock. How one can explain something like this I do not know, except by invoking a spiritual explanation. At the time, religion was not discussed, but Paddy, who was a nominal Roman Catholic, became more involved with his church. Many years later, Fred told me that he had become a committed Christian and active Anglican.

Conclusion

When discussing primal experiences or meeting people who report them, we need to be cautious and not jump to conclusions. It is easy to dismiss such things as ignorance or evil, but the truth is more complex. When I interviewed the brilliant Afrikaner philosopher Professor H. G. Stoker in the 1970s, he told this story. When he was a young student at Potchefstroom University in South Africa in 1914, he had a friend who was homesick. Each Sunday afternoon his friend would go into an open field, known as "the veld," and sit under a particular tree from where he mentally communicated with his twin brother in the town of Uitenhage hundreds of miles away. Stoker explained that the brother also sat under the same type of tree on the family farm. This, he said, was done by telepathy. The tree had something to do with it, even though the student told Stoker that he did not understand what it was. Somehow it amplified the brothers' thoughts.

As a Christian, Professor Stoker found no difficulty accepting this story because he knew it was true. As a skeptical Englishman, I was incredulous. When he saw this, Stoker, with a twinkle in his eye, said that was because I had just arrived in Africa and did not understand the continent or its people. Almost forty years later, I am inclined to agree with him.

Finally, it is worth remembering that the great American philosopher and pastor Jonathan Edwards (1703–1758) was one of the first to record and attempt to explain such experiences in a rational manner. In doing so he steered a Christian path between wild enthusiasm, emotional outburst, and true Christian experiences based on biblical insights. His work is a good starting point for anyone who is seriously worried about such phenomena.[8]

chapter three

Encountering African Traditional Religions

Introduction

In this chapter we explore the logic and meaning of traditional African beliefs and look at reasons why they persist, as well as the response of African Christians to them. Some readers may be shocked by how Christian believers in Africa, and those living in other traditional societies, manage to incorporate beliefs like witchcraft in their Christian worldview. This chapter explains African traditional religions and why this incorporation is not as surprising as it may seem, because it can provide a temporary bridge that enables people to understand their world as it is moved in a new direction through their reading of the Bible.

What Are Traditional Religions?

By traditional religions I mean the type of religion found throughout the world that American anthropologist Robert Redfield called "little traditions." These are religions where primal, or charismatic, experiences, healings, prophecies, visions, and threshold encounters are the principal concern of devotees. In such religions, a shaman, or similar ritual figure, communicates between this world and the next. Often the aim is to placate the ancestors. Redfield contrasted this type of religion with what he called the "Great Traditions," which are religions based on written scriptures with a formalized clergy, or priesthood, and intellectual theology.

As discussed in the previous chapter, at the core of all traditional religions, and many new religious movements, are intense psychic encounters that defy rational explanation. Today the majority of Africans living in nations south of the Sahara are Christians or Muslims. Nevertheless, traditional religions remain important, and there is often an overlap between traditional practices and those of African Christians and Muslims.

The Core Beliefs of African Traditional Religions

When discussing African traditional religions, it is important to recognize that despite the attempts of some scholars to discover an underlying African religion, there are numerous differences between the beliefs and practices of Africans who practice their own traditional religions. These differences correspond to geographic and historical differences between various African communities. As a result, what is true for one group may not be true for another. Generalizations are likely to be wrong.

That being said, there are similarities between different traditional religions throughout Africa, and certain beliefs and practices are common even if the exact way they are understood can vary. The summary offered here is a broad overview that we recognize has limitations.

Ancestors in African traditional religions are not viewed as Europeans view their ancestors or even ghosts. In most African societies, ancestors have some characteristics of ghosts, but they are not considered evil or inherently dangerous. Rather, they are understood to be an integral part of everyday life and concerned for the welfare of their descendants. If family members forget them for too long, though, they can become interfering busybodies because they expect to play a role in the smooth running of society.

Most traditional Africans believe that ancestors continue to live after death in much the same way they lived when they had physical bodies. As a result, they sometimes cause problems for people and can even create misfortune and illness if they turn nasty. This means that when an outbreak of disease occurs or continual misfortune arises, specialists are consulted on how to placate the ancestors. These specialists are people with a calling who have entered their profession after long training and many years of study. As with Western medical specialists, the proof is in the results. If health and good fortune are restored, then it is clear that the traditional healer knows how to communicate with the ancestors whose activity is beyond doubt.

A related aspect of African religions is that they tend to be holistic. That is, they do not make a sharp distinction between this world and the next, or between the secular and the sacred. Within such a framework, primal power exists and is experienced in what may appear to be strange ways.

Fred Welbourn[1] told the story of visiting a village in Uganda where a leopard kept the local people safe and warned them if other leopards were coming to steal their cattle. The villagers visited the leopard's lair without fear of being molested. One day a Makerere University student took Fred to see the leopard. Fred experienced the fright of his life when he realized that at the back of the dark cave the student brought him to was the leopard. It ignored the visitors, and Fred lived to tell the tale.

Africans describe supernatural powers as all-pervasive primal forces that behave very much like electricity. People and things "positively charged" with power can pass it on by contact to anyone who is "negatively charged." Unless this process is properly controlled, damage will result. A positively charged chief might lose some of his power when in contact with a commoner, while the commoner who lacks power is injured by contact with the chief.

When Christians hear such things, they are inclined to dismiss them as superstitions or unbiblical fantasies. Yet the Bible sometimes speaks of power in this way. For example, consider Luke 8:43–47:

> And a woman was there who had been subject to bleeding for twelve years, but no one could heal her. She came up behind him and touched the edge of his cloak, and immediately her bleeding stopped.
>
> "Who touched me?" Jesus asked.
>
> When they all denied it, Peter said, "Master, the people are crowding and pressing against you."
>
> But Jesus said, "Someone touched me; I know that power has gone out from me."
>
> Then the woman, seeing that she could not go unnoticed, came trembling and fell at his feet.

Verses like this are puzzling, but to many Africans they reflect their own experience. They find inspiration in them and see things they believe European missionaries overlook. At its core, the Bible talks about many experiences and realities that resonate with traditional Africans. To recognize these similarities, as African theologian Gabriel Setiloane (1925–2004) points out, Westerners must strip away their rationalistic methods of interpretation.

The atomic structure of matter illuminates the relation between the "natural" and "supernatural." When small children first learn about atoms, they sometimes think that chairs and similar objects, which are described as made of atoms, are dangerous to sit on because one might fall through them. Yet experiences with chairs show they are safe, so children sit on them without hesitation. In everyday life, most people follow commonsense experience with chairs and leave the theory of atoms to experts who can use it to produce electricity or an atomic bomb. So too traditional African societies have experts who can control primal powers. These people are feared and admired. If they use their power to improve their own crops or those of others, their help may be sought. But such a person may also use their power to do harm to others.

Among the Lugbara of Uganda, a man who consistently had better crops than his neighbors could be accused of witchcraft and be punished. Nineteen enterprising young Zulu men who worked in "white towns," such as Pietermaritzburg, and saved their earnings to buy plows were accused of witchcraft. Since the plows enabled them to cultivate more land than their neighbors, their material success was interpreted as "witchcraft."

The Logic of Witchcraft

When European missionaries and colonial officials encountered African witchcraft, they began to see it as proof of the inferiority of Africans. In their view, witchcraft demonstrated that Africans were primitive people who knew nothing of modern science or logical thinking. To bring them into the modern world, Europeans saw it as their task to educate Africans.

This viewpoint was found in both popular culture and numerous early academic writings about Africa. Yet there is a logic to witchcraft beliefs, as anthropologist Edward E. Evans-Pritchard (1902–1973) came to argue in opposition to the accepted view.[2]

Evans-Pritchard based his understanding on fieldwork among the Azande of Sudan. He pointed out that Africans were not stupid. They knew a spark from a fire where they cooked food could fly through the air to land on a thatched roof and burn down a hut. They also knew that sparks often shot up into the air from an open fire, but they rarely burned down nearby huts. Evans-Pritchard argued that knowing the natural cause of a fire was not enough for Africans like the Azande. The big metaphysical question remained unanswered: "Why did this particular spark make it all the way to my hut and why did it catch fire so quickly?"

A system of beliefs identified as "witchcraft" provided the answer. Similarly, a flu epidemic might sweep through an area, and my neighbor might remain perfectly healthy while my family all become ill. Africans knew the medical cause of their illness, especially those who had contact with modern medicine. But the question remained: "Why did we get ill and they did not?" Witchcraft offered an explanation for calamity that went beyond the physical explanation.

What witchcraft does, Evans-Pritchard argued, is answer the underlying "why" question, while common sense and modern science answer the "how" question. Seen in this way, witchcraft has a logic anyone living in a witchcraft society understands, a logic that incorporates personal conflict between people and psychic causes that lie behind surface causes. Witchcraft gives meaning to events that are otherwise meaningless.

Evans-Pritchard and other social anthropologists who accepted his arguments went on to note that the exact nature of witchcraft, sorcery, and various forms of healing differed from society to society. Yet the basic logic remained the same and gave traditional beliefs an enduring appeal.

Traditional Beliefs and Modern Medicine

The changing attitudes of traditional Africans to modern medicine can be summed up by the following story. In the 1970s, tuberculosis reached epidemic proportions in an area of South Africa's Transkei region. This happened even though it had a teaching hospital funded by the Dutch Reformed Church and staffed by excellent doctors. The problem was that most Africans who contracted tuberculosis first went to see local healers before visiting the "white hospital." By the time they came to the hospital, months or sometimes years after contracting the disease, it was much harder, if not impossible, to treat.

To overcome this problem, the hospital devised a scheme to cooperate with local African healers instead of condemning them. Africans, even in rural areas, knew illnesses were the result of infections caused by bacteria and viruses. Yet the question of what had caused a bacteria or virus to attack a particular person and not someone else remained. Traditional healers derived answers from witchcraft, and sufferers turned to them for freedom from the spiritual forces that had caused their illness before going to the hospital to get treatment for physical symptoms. Since timing was crucial in treating tuberculosis, the hospital gained the confidence of local African healers by involving them in diagnosing and treating diseases. This meant recognizing that traditional healers had a role to play in the healing process and could often successfully treat minor illnesses, like the common cold, by providing counseling to patients.

This campaign of mutual respect and cooperation provided free training to local healers to help them recognize the symptoms of tuberculosis and other infectious diseases. Traditional healers were then encouraged to send their patients to the hospital for a medical examination as quickly as possible. Healers were also given a role in helping patients diagnosed with tuberculosis to cope with their condition. The approach worked well and played a major role in reducing tuberculosis and other infectious diseases in the area.

The case of Estelle, a Zulu woman and important traditional healer in South Africa, further illustrates the possibility of working with people who embrace traditional beliefs without demanding that they renounce them. In explaining why she became a healer, Estelle said that as a young woman, she had suffered severe migraines that Western doctors failed to control. Eventually, because her health was affecting her work, she sought help from a traditional Zulu diviner even though she was a baptized Christian and active in her church.

The diviner cured her headaches and said her ancestors had called her to become a healer. In a series of dreams, Estelle's ancestors told her she must not wear Western shoes or enter a church building.

She then underwent years of rigorous training before becoming a respected healer who helped people by practicing the old ways of healing.

Estelle said her ancestors told her to remain a Christian even though she was told not to enter a church building because they found the inside of churches "frightening." Yet Estelle made sure that her children and grandchildren went to church and became baptized believers. This story does not fit well with the division between Christianity and traditional religions that most Christians uphold. It is shared here not as a spiritual model to emulate, but rather to illustrate the complexity of living situations in areas where African traditional religions remain valued and the kinds of compromises made to accommodate them.

Learning the Lessons of Surprising Conversions

It is easy as a Christian to look at the way Africans practice their religions and see the evils of syncretism at work in people like Estelle. Yet this reaction fails to enter the thought world of Africans who may be sincere Christian believers even as they seek to incorporate aspects of traditional African life and belief into their lives.

This does not mean we should embrace every instance of accommodation to traditional beliefs. We must carefully consider what the Bible teaches before engaging. In this way, Western Christians can begin to gain the trust of African traditional believers and members of African independent churches, which are now the largest group of Christians in Africa, and interact with them in meaningful ways.

Early Christian evangelists in Europe faced similar challenges. In his *History of the English Church and People*, the Venerable Bede, the first historian of European Christianity, tells how Pope Gregory I advised evangelizing the pagan English.[3] Pagan idols were to be destroyed, but the temples they stood in were well built and ought to be preserved. They could be purified with prayer and holy water to allow them to be used as churches. Pagan holidays were to be avoided, but to prevent the children of recent converts from seeing Christianity as a killjoy religion, new holidays ought to be encouraged.

Many today may regard this type of advice with skepticism. Tom Paine made fun of it in his *Age of Reason* as a compromise with paganism. But the approach appears to have been effective, as Richard Fletcher points out in his fascinating book *The Barbarian Conversion: From Paganism to Christianity*.[4] Some people cast doubt on the sincerity of early British converts, ignoring the fact that these people and their descendants were willing to die for their faith.

Although the conversion stories of African Christians may not fit the image Western believers have of what it means to become a Christian, there are ample examples of African converts and their children living and dying for their faith. We Westerners should learn to approach them with humility, allowing God to teach us through such encounters. We can learn much about successful evangelism by hearing their stories.

chapter four

Africa's Forgotten Christian Heritage

Introduction

One of the best ways Christians can engage Africans and people of African descent is by recognizing the rich and largely forgotten Christian heritage of Africa. For example, Martin Luther corresponded with and, in 1534, met Michael the Deacon, an African minister from Ethiopia. Michael, for whom Luther had great respect, visited him in the German town of Wittenberg.

Michael belonged to the ancient Coptic Church of Ethiopia.[1] Luther made no secret of his admiration for African Christianity. Yet until recently, this part of Luther's story was overlooked by church historians. What follows is an outline of some of the key developments in the long history of African Christianity.

Africa's Forgotten Christian Heritage

In Acts 8:26–39 we read the story of the first non-Palestinian convert to Christianity. He is described as an "Ethiopian eunuch" who was "an important official in charge of all the treasury of the Kandake (which means 'queen of the Ethiopians')." His conversion was the beginning of Christianity in Africa. This means that the Christian church was established in Africa long before it was in England or in most of the Roman world. One of the remarkable facts about Christianity is that most early Christian leaders were Africans. Today many are known as the "early church fathers."

According to Clement of Alexandria (150–215 AD), after the execution of the apostle Peter in Rome, his companion Mark moved to Alexandria, where he too was martyred around 68 AD. Before that he planted Christianity in the great Greco-Roman city of Alexandria. From there it spread south along the Nile, where a growing number of people, who became known as Copts, embraced the gospel during the second century AD, while at the same time developing their own distinct language, Coptic.

Clement was the first great Christian theologian whose school provided Christians with both a philosophical response to Roman paganism and an example to follow in terms of practical living in a corrupt world. Later, Clement's work was developed by Origen (185–254 AD), who became the greatest philosophical theologian of the early church. Origen's great contribution to the growth of the church was his *Hexapla*, a carefully constructed volume of Scripture that showed the Hebrew text of the Old Testament alongside four Greek translations. He also grounded Christian thought in the work of earlier Jewish philosophers such as Philo of Alexandria and strongly resisted the growth of heresies, such as the emerging Gnostic tradition that distorted the clear teachings of Scripture.

It was in Egypt that the heresy of Arianism took root through the work of Arius, who had a knack for popularizing his teachings in popular songs and sayings. He courted the masses but was resisted by Athanasius (296–373 AD), the bishop of Alexandria, who defended Christian orthodoxy's definitive shape. Athanasius suffered persecution for his solid defense of Trinitarian Christianity and was exiled five times by the Roman emperor. He left his mark on the entire church and is remembered in what today is called the Athanasian Creed, which is one of the three great Christian creeds.

Importantly, Athanasius consecrated a young Ethiopian priest as bishop of Aksum, in Ethiopia. This priest returned home to Ethiopia and played a key role in organizing the already existing Ethiopian church deep inside sub-Saharan Africa. Athanasius's great successor, Cyril of Alexandria, was a staunch supporter of Trinitarian Christianity who is regarded by the Ethiopian Orthodox Church as the "teacher *par excellence*." Ever since Cyril, the Ethiopian church has based its theological teachings on his main doctrinal writings.

From Egypt, Christianity spread along the coast of North Africa, where all of the great cities quickly developed flourishing Christian churches. Places like Hippo, the birthplace of St. Augustine (354–430 AD), were particularly important as Christianity spread into Europe. North African church leaders stimulated the development of European thought, as the standard histories of Christianity acknowledge. What is often overlooked is that most of these early Christian thinkers were black Africans, as can be seen from their places of birth and the earliest artistic depictions of them. Today students of theology may tend to view them, erroneously, as though they were Europeans.

The age of the church fathers included periods of intense persecution, beginning in AD 284 with the persecutions of the Roman emperor Diocletian. The first great Christian martyr under Diocletian was Peter, the bishop of Alexandria. Farther along the Nile, whole communities of Coptic Christians were destroyed by Roman legions. Christians fled into the deserts of Egypt and surrounding countries, including Nubia, to escape persecution and to pray for the church. One of the most well known of those who fled to the desert, at least in terms of his historical impact, was St. Anthony (251–356 AD). His example inspired the monastic movement, which played a key role in the evangelization of pagan Europe for many centuries.

The Spread of Global Christianity

African Christianity flourished following the conversion of the peoples of Egypt and North Africa bordering the Mediterranean Sea. By the seventh century AD, the population of Egypt and surrounding countries was almost 100 percent Christian. From Egypt and the Arabian Peninsula, Christianity had spread into Asia as part of the first great expansion of Christianity that reached India and eventually China, using trade networks along which Christians spread their faith, as the map below shows:

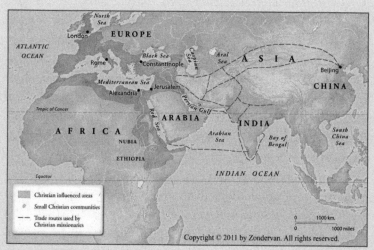

The early Christian world to the sixth century. Here it is important to note the existence of the African kingdoms of Nubia and Ethiopia, which are normally left off maps of the early Christian world. It should also be noted that by the sixth century, Christianity had spread along trade routes to both China and India. Although we know little about these early Christian communities, we know they did exist.

Christian missionaries and traders from Egypt, Arabia, and Ethiopia evangelized the lands south of Egypt's ancient border city of Swenett from the fourth century AD onward. Today Swenett is known as Aswan and is famous for the great dam on the Nile that takes its name. This area and what lay south of it were part of ancient Nubia, most of which is part of today's Sudan. Nubia itself was an ancient civilization stretching back to around 2500 BC, a major trading partner of ancient Egypt, and a source of rich minerals mined there.

Christians established a vibrant church in Nubia and a society that left behind many artistic treasures and archaeological remains, like the wall painting from a cave church shown on this page.

The Nubians maintained trade and cultural ties with Egypt and Ethiopia to such a degree that in addition to their own African language, they made extensive use of Greek. As a result, the Nubian elite were literate in both Nubian and Greek. All of this changed with the rise of Islam and the Arab conquest of Egypt, North Africa, and most of Spain in the seventh century AD.

The remarkably rapid Arab conquests were possible because lands they conquered in North Africa had enjoyed peace for hundreds of years as part of the Roman and Byzantine Empires. They were lightly defended by armies

Source: LeGabrie/WikiCommons

that were more like local police forces than military machines. The immediate effect of the Arab conquests was that both Nubia and Ethiopia were cut off from Christian Europe. Over time these Christian kingdoms were largely forgotten in Europe, which was fighting for its own survival against Arab and Viking invaders.

From the time of their conversion until the destruction of the last Nubian kingdom around 1450 AD, there were two flourishing Christian civilizations in the heart of Africa, Nubia and Ethiopia.

From the seventh century on, Nubians and Ethiopians faced and repelled repeated Arab invasions. We do not know what led to the final downfall of Christian Nubia, although Ethiopia survived as an independent country until the present. Archaeological evidence suggests Nubian Christianity was destroyed by a combination of invasion from Egypt and constant raids from the west by nomads who had converted to Islam.

By the end of the fifteenth century, Nubia no longer existed. Its towns and cities, its churches and monasteries were either destroyed or simply depopulated and left to be buried under the sands of the desert. Gradually a new Islamic state, the Sudan, emerged.

Farther south and to the east, the equally ancient kingdom of Ethiopia was more mountainous and better able to resist Islamic conquest, making it the oldest continually existing Christian civilization in the world. Today the African people of Ethiopia can claim a longer history as a Christian society than any other country.

The Devastating Impact of Islamic Invasions on Global Christianity

The impact of Arab invasions on Africa in general, and Christianity in particular, is impossible to exaggerate. Before these rapid invasions occurred, Christians shared a common culture and heritage even if they sometimes violently disagreed on issues of doctrine and practice. This culture extended from the Scottish borders to the Black Sea and Africa, and from there it traveled to faraway places.

Once Islam was firmly established in the Middle East and along the coast of North Africa, these routes were cut and, if not completely closed, became very hazardous. Communication between European Christians and Christians living in other parts of the world, including Africa, ceased. This communications blackout lasted until the so-called "Age of Discovery" in the sixteenth century. The following map illustrates how Muslim lands isolated African Christian kingdoms from Europe:

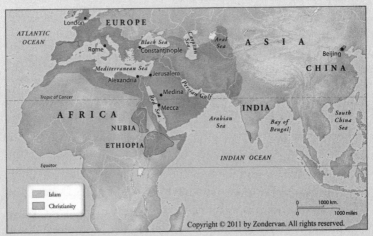

African Christian kingdoms isolated from Europe by Muslim lands

The Impact of the Slave Trade on Africa

In Africa the impact of Islamic conquest was magnified by the fact that the coastal areas along the Red Sea and what is today Somalia came under Arab control. Over the centuries, Arab rule extended as far south as Zanzibar. Arab North Africa as well as the east coast facing the Indian Ocean became centers of the Arab slave trade that devastated African kingdoms south of the Sahara.

Today when people talk about the slave trade, they automatically think of the trans-Atlantic slave trade that began in the sixteenth century and continued until the early nineteenth. In those centuries, a shocking number of Africans, between five and ten million or even fifteen million, were kidnapped and transported to the Americas. Many died en route.

What this story overlooks is the Arab slave trade in Africa that began in the seventh century and continues today. The number of Africans sold into slavery is difficult to estimate because, unlike the trans-Atlantic slave trade, detailed records of the capture and sale of slaves in the Arab slave trade are lacking. In his popular television series, *The Africans*, and its accompanying book,[2] Ali Mazrui (1933–2014) dismisses the Arab slave trade as insignificant by asking where the descendants of the slaves are today. The answer is that, as Ronald Segal points out, there is extensive evidence that Arab traders regularly castrated male slaves and often killed the babies of female slaves.[3]

Ronald Segal suggests that the total number of black Africans sold into slavery in northern slave markets or along the East African coast by Muslim slavers between 700 and 1900 AD was about 14 million. He notes that this figure is deceptive in terms of the total number of Africans captured by or killed by slavers. There is solid evidence that large numbers of African captives died on the long trek to slave markets or were killed resisting capture. Evidence suggests that around ten Africans died for every one who was eventually sold into slavery.[4] This means the total number of Africans whose lives were destroyed by slavers could rise to nearly 150 million.

Although the impact of Arab slave raids on African societies is hard to estimate, there is some well-recorded evidence. For example, in the fifteenth century, Portuguese missionaries reached the Kingdom of the Congo, which they described as very similar in its social organization and economy to contemporary kingdoms in Europe. Within a hundred years of the arrival of the missionaries, the kingdom was weakened by civil war, followed by Arab slave raids from which the area never recovered.[5]

During the eighteenth century, the evangelical revival in Europe and America saw African slavery as anti-Christian and began an extended campaign for its abolition. Former slavers like John New-ton (1725–1807), who is best remembered for writing the hymn "Amazing Grace," became some of slavery's most vocal critics. The campaign led to the abolition of slavery in British territories in 1833 and resulted in the Royal Navy patrolling the coast of Africa to inter-cept slave ships and free their captives. After a bitter civil war, slavery was abolished in the United States of America in 1865.[6]

The anti-slavery movement helped create the nineteenth-century missionary movement, which inspired people like David Livingstone (1813–1873). Livingstone and other missionaries had their weak-nesses, yet their work led to the abolition of the internal African slave trade, as journalist Henry Stanley (1841–1904) observed.

The tragic history of the slave trade, however, is only one of the factors that shaped later European attitudes toward Africans. The other great influences were the Enlightenment and the theory of evolution.

African Christianity before the Enlightenment

Although some have argued that racism goes back to antiquity, in the Greco-Roman world skin color and what we call "race" were unimportant.[7] The non-racial attitude of the Greco-Roman world continued for many cen-turies and deeply influenced the

St. Maurice's statue created around 1250 AD in Magdeburg Dom (Cathedral), Germany. He is dressed as a contemporary military officer and shows an African who was regarded as a great lord alongside Europeans of similar rank.
Source: Photograph by Irving Hexham

development of Europe, where black Africans were held in high regard, as sculptures and paintings of people like St. Maurice show. Many statues of a similar kind are found in the great cathedrals of Europe. Africans are also frequently found in paintings of the nativity where one of the three kings is almost always black. These works of art were intended to instruct Christians and make no negative distinction in terms of skin color or race.

As late as the eighteenth century, Anton Wilhelm Amo (1703–1759), a native of Ghana, gained a reputation as a rationalist philosopher in Germany. After completing his degree at the University of Halle in 1727, he obtained his doctorate from the University of Wittenberg in 1734 and was appointed lecturer in philosophy at the University of Halle.[8] Amo is just one example of Africans who held respected positions in Europe prior to the Enlightenment.[9] All of this changed in the eighteenth century when public intellectuals in Europe, most of whom held university chairs, began to write world histories that rejected Christianity.

Africa, the Enlightenment, and Scientific Racism

It is usual to regard the Enlightenment as a period of social reform, scientific development, and progress. Yet it was anything but progressive for black Africans. A good case can be made that modern racism originated during the Enlightenment.[10]

French philosopher François-Marie Arouet (1694–1778), better known as Voltaire, set the tone for Enlightenment attitudes toward Africans. Derogatory remarks about blacks can be found throughout his writing. In his short essay *The Negro*, he sums up his racist outlook, observing: "The NEGRO race is a species of men as different from ours as the breed of spaniels is from that of greyhounds. . . . If their understanding is not of a different nature from ours, it is at least greatly inferior. They are not capable of any great application or association of ideas." Voltaire advocated polygenesis, or the separate creation of different human races.[11]

Other public intellectuals of the time, such as Scottish philosopher David Hume (1711–1776), best known for his criticisms of arguments for belief in God, reinforced Enlightenment attitudes toward Africans,[12] as did Jean Jacques Rousseau (1712–1778), who is remembered for his attack on slavery. He spoke quite freely about "negroes and savages," making it clear that his "savages" are identified with Africans. Immanuel Kant (1724–1804) was more cautious, but thought that racial mixture was to be discouraged and laid a foundation for segregation. Finally, Hegel (1770–1831) had no hesitation in saying, "The Negro . . . exhibits the natural man in his completely wild and untamed state. . . . At this point we leave Africa to mention it no more. For it is no historical part of the World."[13] Such examples demonstrate racist views about Africans that were propagated during the Enlightenment and help to explain the general ignorance of Africa in nineteenth-century Europe that in some respects continues even today.

Charles Darwin (1809–1882) and his theory of evolution was also used as an explanation for racial differences and social development. This is clearly seen in the records of the British Colonial Office, which, until the publication of *On the Origin of the Species* in 1859, wrote about non-European peoples with considerable respect. Until then Africans were referred to as nations with their own emperors, kings, and princes. After 1860 the tone changed, downgrading Africans as their societies became "tribes" and their leaders "chiefs."

Whatever the merits of the biological theory of evolution, its social impact was disastrous. Prior to its development, supporters of slavery used the grotesque argument that Africans could be enslaved because they lacked souls. Now the argument was given a "scientific" twist. Africans were not normal humans. They were subhumans who were closer to apes.

Although most Christian leaders rejected such language, it nevertheless had a profound effect on the way Africans were viewed. As ideas about social evolution spread, it became a "scientific fact" that Africans lacked intelligence. By the 1880s and 1890s, missionaries who had spent decades in Africa were debating "scientists" in public meetings, for example at the Anthropological Institute in London, where scholars argued that their efforts in Africa were a waste of time because Africans lacked basic intelligence. Scientific racism was on the rise and was abandoned only after it was systematically applied to a wide range of people by the Nazis.[14]

Missionary Evaluations of Africans

Most nineteenth-century missionaries who worked in Africa had great respect for Africans. They argued that Africans lacked the technological achievements of Europeans because of geographic isolation and the impact of the Arab slave trade. The positive attitude toward Africans of Alan Gardiner (1794–1851), the first missionary to the Zulu of South Africa, is representative of the outlook of most missionaries.

Of course, there were counterexamples. Robert Moffat (1795–1883), the father-in-law of David Livingstone (1813–1873), has been accused of calling Africans dirty, lazy people. This claim is based on his comments about a village in Botswana. In context, however, his journal shows that these negative comments were made against a background of praise for other villages, whose people had warned him about the residents of this particular village.

Missionaries to Africa during the nineteenth century generally raised Africans above what the Victorians called "the great unwashed." These were the inhabitants of English towns who lacked education and lived in drunken squalor, surviving on a diet of gin and potatoes. Africans, in the view of the majority of missionaries, were more intelligent and socially advanced than these poor, disadvantaged people.[15]

Many missionaries to Africa expressed their astonishment at finding what they thought were Christian and/or Jewish features embedded in traditional African societies. Alan Gardiner was convinced that the Zulu were Jews who over time had forgotten their heritage largely because the climate of Africa had destroyed their Scriptures. Over a century later, after spending many years in Uganda teaching at Makerere University and studying the traditional religion of Buganda, Fred Welbourn (1912–1986) expressed his astonishment that the traditional priests of the Buganda made the Orthodox sign of the cross during religious ceremonies. He speculated that they must have been influenced by Coptic Christianity, but as a scholar he could find no evidence for what seemed a very strange coincidence.

Twentieth-century scholars dismissed such possible links as the fantasies of missionaries and religious fanatics who failed to recognize the true nature of African society. All claims to a Christian or Jewish heritage were dismissed until 1996 when DNA tests supported the claim of the Lemba of southern Africa to be Jews.[16] Although some scholars still question this result, all agree that the Lemba have "a Middle Eastern genetic history."[17]

Until more extensive genetic results are available for the whole of sub-Saharan Africa, it is unwise to speculate. Whatever is the case genetically, the Christian heritage of Africa is ancient and rich.

Conclusion

So what does this history have to do with today? The answer is that in the third quarter of the nineteenth century, missionaries in Africa began reporting about converts who danced, sought healing, produced new music, and spoke in strange tongues. Today it is clear that these people were the forerunners of the American Azusa Street

Revival of 1906 and that African converts, taken overseas on mission trips, spread African forms of worship that other Christians embraced. This is most clearly seen in the birth of the charismatic movement in the mid-1960s. It grew out of the work of South African Pentecostal preacher David du Plessis (1905–1987), who was strongly influenced by Zulu Christianity. The charismatic revival shows that African influences on global Christianity are alive and well today.[18]

Knowing this history allows Christians to develop a rapport with Africans who belong to missionary churches such as the Anglicans and Presbyterians, as well as members of African independent, or indigenous, churches that were founded by African leaders who are often described as "prophets." It also helps us talk to the much smaller number of Africans who continue to practice traditional religions. Such people often see Christianity as alien to African tradition. Once they realize that Christianity is an African religion, they may not become Christians, but they will be far more open to the gospel and willing to take Christianity seriously.

chapter five

The Essence of Yogic Religions

Introduction

Buddhism, Hinduism, Jainism, and a variety of related religious traditions are identified here as "Yogic religions" because at their core is the practice of one or another form of yoga that seeks some form of escape or liberation from this world. Although there are major differences between the different Yogic religions, they all assume that this world is a veil of sorrow that must be endured until some form of escape becomes possible.

A. C. Bhaktivedanta Swami Prabhupada (1896–1977), the founder of the Hare Krishna movement, a movement that became well known in Europe and North America in the 1960s, summed up the negativity toward the world of Yogic traditions when he said, "This place is not meant for happiness. . . . It is a place of miseries and . . . is temporary."[1] The great twentieth-century Buddhist scholar Edward Conze (1904–1979) wrote, "The Buddhist point of view will appeal only to those people who are completely disillusioned with the world as it is, and with themselves, who are extremely sensitive to pain, suffering, and any kind of turmoil, who have an extreme desire for happiness, and a considerable capacity for renunciation. . . . The Buddhist seeks for a total happiness beyond this world."[2]

To many Westerners, the Yogic view of the human condition may seem pessimistic, but practitioners disagree and see it as both realistic and hopeful. They believe it offers eventual relief from the human condition. Mircea Eliade, a Romanian scholar who played a key role in establishing religious studies in America, stated that Yogic soteriological doctrines "may appear pessimistic to Westerners, for whom personality remains, in the last analysis, the foundation of all morality and mysticism. But, for India, what matters most is not so much the salvation of the *personality* as obtaining *absolute freedom.*"[3]

Yogic religions portray a very different view of our condition and the solution to human problems than do the Abramic religions (discussed in later chapters), which see the patriarch Abraham as the founder of faith.[4] These religions, which include Judaism, Christianity, and Islam, place primary value on the relationship of humans to a creator God while emphasizing the salvation of the individual. Yogic religions promote a form of salvation that involves an escape from individuality. Ninian Smart summed up the Yogic outlook when he wrote:

> Men and other living beings are continually being reborn. With death, the individual is reborn in a different form. This everlasting recurrence of births and deaths can only be stopped by transcending it by attaining a liberation in a transcendental sphere where the self is freed from mental and bodily encumbrances. Typically, this is achieved by the practice of austerity and yoga: self-denial and self-discipline are means of destroying that which leads to rebirth-Karma.[5]

From this quotation it is clear that if we are to understand Yogic religions, we need to know what is meant by certain key terms and how they relate to each other in the Yogic worldview. It is also helpful to understand the historical origins of the Yogic tradition.

The Creators of Our Image of India

Most textbooks on world religions reproduce a fairly standard account of the history of the Yogic tradition, based on the works of scholars who initially worked for the British East India Company (BEIC). In this context, young men like Charles Wilkins (1749–1836) and William Jones (1746–1794) were tasked by the company with making the cultural traditions of India available to employees and the broader world. This was not an altruistic aim. Rather, it reflected the BEIC's policy of educating its officers on the traditions of the people they worked among as a means of negotiating effectively and ruling without unnecessary friction.

Wilkins and Jones played a key role in creating the Asiatic Society for the study of Indian history and culture as well as translating key texts into English. Wilkins, for example, produced the first translation of the *Bhagavad Gita* in any European language and went on to produce many other translations as well as dictionaries of Indian languages. Jones, who worked as a judge in Bengal, revitalized the study of Sanskrit, which had fallen into disuse during the long centuries of Muslim rule. He also developed the theory of the relationship of Sanskrit to European languages. Both men were fascinated by India and worked to gain respect for Indian history and culture.

A different approach was taken by James Mill (1773–1836), the father of well-known philosopher John Stuart Mill (1806–1873). He published what for many years was the definitive history of India. This work despised Hindu culture, which he saw as superstitious and corrupt, while promoting Indian Islam as a superior religion and culture. His works provided a framework for understanding Indian history that still lingers today.

With this history in mind, we will survey the key concepts in Yogic religions. It is important to remember that considerable variations may be found within the Yogic traditions.

Karma

Karma is the key to understanding Yogic religions. At its crudest, karma is viewed as a physical substance that literally sticks to people's consciousness, or soul, binding them to the material world. It is the cosmic law of cause and effect that ensures that whatever a person does, good or bad, has ultimate consequences. If we do good, we produce good karma. If we do evil, we produce bad karma. Good karma frees people from the illusions of the material world and makes the hope of liberation possible. Bad karma binds people to the world as it creates illusions of happiness.

Probably the earliest systematic discussion of karma is found in the ancient *Brhadaranyaka Upanisad*, which, it is claimed, was composed as an oral text around 700 BC and written down after the tenth century AD. The earliest extant copy is dated to 1600 AD. This document's teachings provide a good summary of the way karma is widely understood. In a key passage, it reads: "[A]ccording as one acts, according as one conducts himself, so does he become. The doer of good becomes good. The doer of evil becomes evil. One becomes virtuous by virtuous action, bad by bad action."

In the foreword to his translation of the *Bhagavad Gita*, A. C. Bhaktivedanta Swami Prabhupada explains the action of karma as follows:

> Suppose I am a businessman and have worked very hard with intelligence and have amassed a great bank balance. Then I am an enjoyer. But then say I have lost all my money in business; then I am a sufferer. Similarly, in every field of life we enjoy the results of our works, or we suffer the results. This is called karma.[6]

Rebirth

Closely related to the idea of karma is rebirth. In the Yogic traditions, rebirth is explained in two ways. Most Hindus believe that when human beings die, their soul enters another body. Technically this is known as transmigration. Buddhists, on the other hand, typically believe that our sense of personhood comes from sense impressions that create the illusion that a person experiences them. But for Buddhists, there is no person, soul, or spirit. Buddhists postulate reincarnation, rather than transmigration. Reincarnation means the continuation of sense impressions without an experiencing person.

Within Yogic religions, karma and rebirth are brought together through belief in an endless chain of existence. This is known as samsara.

Samsara, Maya, Dharma, and Moksha

Samsara, or the "wheel of existence," is the name given to a vast network of births and deaths through endless lifetimes involving incarnations in many worlds, heavens, and hells. Yogic religions teach that every thing and every being are bound together in the infinite repetition of birth and death, bound together through karma and rebirth.

Ordinarily people do not experience the bonds of karma or become aware of the wheel of existence. Instead they experience their lives as a fleeting moment of consciousness to which they ascribe ultimate significance. But this awareness of one's individuality and belief in the significance of one's present life is an illusion. The illusory nature of experience, or what is normally called "reality," is brought about by *maya*. This originally meant "the creative and transforming power of a god." Over time the term came to be understood as "illusion" and plays an important role in Hindu philosophy and popular religion, especially the modern philosophical system of Vedanta where the world is seen as essentially unreal. The term conjures up an illusory universe. Once we recognize the illusionary nature of existence, we realize we need to be liberated from it. This means release from samsara and the bonds of karma.

In Hinduism, *dharma* is a religious way of life that embraces all one does and all of society. Dharma implies the idea of a fixed standard of divine conduct that is a sacred law by which human beings must live.

Liberation consists of freeing oneself, or being freed, from the bonds of karma and experiencing release from samsara. This form of salvation is known as *moksha*. Moksha takes many different forms in various Hindu traditions. As a result, it can be experienced in a confusing number of ways. For example, it can be experienced as absorption into the whole, union with god or the gods, entry into life with a particular god such as Krishna, or simply annihilation.

In Buddhism, liberation is called *nirvana*. What nirvana is, Buddhists cannot say, because all anyone can know is this world of cause and effect. Nirvana, on the other hand, is not conditioned by anything in our universe or by cause and effect; it is beyond comprehension. All Buddhists can do is affirm belief in it. Yet it can be understood that nirvana is freedom from the wheel of samsara and the bonds of karma and is the cessation of our present mode of existence.

The classic story that describes nirvana is a man who comes to a river that is so wide he cannot see the other side. Yet he knows that where he is living is unsafe and he must cross the river. He builds a raft and floats across the river in the hope that things will be better. Yet he really does not know, nor can he say, what he will encounter.

Astrology

Many Western scholars have chosen to ignore the magical aspects of Yogic religions. For example, between 1912 and 1942 more than twenty books were published on Buddhism by Caroline A. F. Rhys-Davids (1857–1942), who held academic appointments at Manchester University and then at the University of London's School of African and Oriental Studies in London. More recently, between 1920 and 1978, the British barrister Christmas Humphreys (1901–1983) wrote more than thirty books on Buddhism. Both authors presented Buddhism as highly rationalistic, although toward the end of her life, Rhys-Davids turned personally to Spiritualism. As both writers were best-selling authors, their works had a major impact on the reception of Buddhism in the West.

Popular writers on the Hindu tradition, including Monier Monier-Williams (1819–1899) and others, downplayed the role of astrology and related magical practices in the Hindu tradition. Yet such practices are an essential part of Hinduism and other Yogic traditions.

More recent scholars such as Edward Conze (1904–1979) and Mircea Eliade (1907–1986), who were more deeply involved in the practice of Yogic religions, have rightly drawn attention to the magical aspects of Yogic religions and particularly to the importance of belief in astrology.[7] Eliade points out that belief in astrology arises naturally from belief in karma and rebirth. In the West, astrology is accepted today largely by people who believe it works rather than because of its relationship to other beliefs. However, astrology reinforces belief in such things as karma by linking the time of one's birth, which is understood as a rebirth, with what a person did in their past lives, and it dramatizes Yogic beliefs generally.

Historically, belief in astrology was widespread in the Greco-Roman world. It declined with the rise of Christianity and was ridiculed by early Christian writers. Astrological ideas were revived during the sixteenth-century Renaissance, but these ideas were severely criticized by both Protestant Reformers and leaders of the Catholic Counter-Reformation. By the time of the Enlightenment in the eighteenth century, European astrology had virtually died out. In the nineteenth century, it was generally regarded as a failed science.

Outside of the Western world, in India, China, and the Islamic world, astrology retained much of its popularity with little serious criticism because it links the individual (or in Buddhism, sense perceptions) to a cosmic order. In Yogic religions, everything depends on one's past, which, like the present, is shaped by karma, the eternal law of cause and effect. Where astrology is accepted in Islam—and not all Muslims accept it—a person's fate is inevitably linked to the inscrutable will of God, which is somehow indicated in their astrological signs.

The Meaning of Yoga

Yogic beliefs and the practice of yoga in various forms unify Yogic religions. But what is yoga? Today, yoga is thought of as "a way of life," "an experience," "healthy exercise," and simply "a way of meditation." All of these descriptions are correct. Eliade explains that "etymologically *yoga* derives from the root *yuj*, 'to bind together, hold fast, yoke. . . .' The word *yoga* serves, in general, to describe any *ascetic technique* and any *method of meditation*."[8] These techniques, Conze argued, allow practitioners to gain control of first the body and then the mind.

Meditation or yoga can be described as an inward journey on which the meditator leaves behind the rational mind and enters a new realm of consciousness. There are many forms of yoga, all of which involve the concentration of the mind, breathing exercises, or devotional activities such as the dances and chants of groups like the Hare Krishna movement.

Such meditation affects people differently, and effects are modified by the particular beliefs the meditator holds. The religions of the Yogic tradition all view yoga as a step toward release from the bonds of karma, which ultimately will lead to liberation from the endlessness of samsara.

In attempting to understand the traditional impact of yoga, it is important to note that words cannot fully express what the meditator experiences. One can experience meditation and its results, they say, but it is impossible to describe them fully to another person. What we can say with assurance is that when meditators attempt to describe their experiences, they repeatedly depict states of consciousness we might associate with primal experiences and the use of drugs.

The Yogic System

Yogic beliefs flow from a holistic vision of the universe, a multi-million-year perspective that modern advocates of Yogic traditions associate with the theory of evolution. Behind this modern understanding of yoga is the assumption that our material world is illusory because true reality exists on a different, nonmaterial plane. True reality is essentially non-dualistic, which means that "there is complete identity between the 'self and the one' Power" that "sustains the cosmos," as the Hindu philosopher Shankara (788–820 AD) argued, meaning that the apparent multiplicity of life and selves is an illusion.[9] In the West, this view developed in the early nineteenth century to become what is known as monism. Many schools of philosophy in India, Japan, and other Eastern nations promote the essential oneness of everything, or nondualism. One can find elements of materialism and other views playing a strong role in the Yogic tradition, and historically, following the Indian philosopher Ramamuja (1017–1137 AD), there was a school of "qualified non-dualism" in Hinduism in India that made room for individual selves to worship the one, in what became known as Bhakti,[10] or devotional movements like the Hare Krishna movement.

The Yogic tradition conceives of the human plight as essentially an ontological problem, a matter of our fundamental being and our belief in individuality. Humans are delivered from individuality when they lose their identity and consciousness of personhood. As Eliade puts it, "The wretchedness of human life is not owing to divine punishment or to an original sin, but to *ignorance* . . . metaphysical ignorance."[11] Life is wretched because we experience it as separation, and we will continue to do so until we understand and experience the oneness of all things, until we merge with the Absolute.

Practitioners of yoga maintain that discipline is the means by which one can regain one's true ontological status and lose individual personhood. Because such discipline and the practice of yoga are difficult, one needs the guidance of a guru.

The Guru

A *guru* is a person who has been initiated into the spiritual world and is able to help the uninitiated. Peter Brent gives a vivid account of gurus in his book *Godmen of India*.[12] He shows that the guru demands an inflexible relationship in which the disciple surrenders totally to his authority. Gurus teach and facilitate. They have gone before and experienced the terrors of psychological disorientation that meditation can bring. In the language of Yogic religion, the guru encounters spiritual beings, battles demons, and embraces gods. Each guru shares a tradition with other gurus, and none speaks for himself or herself. Each guru has his or her own guru, living or dead, so that a succession of teachers share esoteric knowledge and communicate ancient techniques of psychic spirituality.

Gurus are not prophets who declare the will of God and appeal to propositions found in a sacred book. Rather, they are said to be greater than God because they lead to God. Gurus have shared the essence of the Absolute and experienced the oneness of being, which endows them with divine powers and the ability to master people and things in this world.

In the Hindu tradition, the true guru is held to be a god-man with superhuman powers and is recognized as a sacred being. For example, members of the Hare Krishna movement, who are followers of the late A. C. Bhaktivedanta Swami Prabhupada, claim that their deceased guru has ascended to the spiritual world, where he has become a god.

There is evidence that some gurus have had sexual relations with their male and female followers. Such relationships are viewed in terms of tantric practices, taught within some branches of the Yogic system as a path to liberation. Originally *tantra* referred to the reading of sacred texts, but over time it took on its modern meaning, which is the attainment of enlightenment through the use of rituals of a magical and sexual nature.

Yogic Exercises as Yogic Propaganda

As we saw earlier, interest in the Yogic tradition was promoted by the Theosophical Society in the late nineteenth century. Earlier, some German philosophers, such as Arthur Schopenhauer (1788–1860), were fascinated by what they heard about Hinduism, but it was not until the late nineteenth century that Swami Vivekananda (1863–1902) began to popularize Hindu religious thought and practices in the West. Later, D. T. Suzuki performed a similar task by popularizing Buddhism.

The promotion of Yogic religions began in earnest with the World's Congress of Religions held in Chicago in 1893.[13] There, Vivekananda made a major impact on his audience with sophisticated arguments and his winning personality. He presented Hinduism as a religion in tune with modern science.[14] A similar case for Buddhism was presented by the less well-known Hewavitarane Dharmapala (1864–1933).[15] Both men can be described as the first global missionaries of the Yogic tradition and were supported by Theosophists.[16]

More than fifty years later, Richard Hittleman (1927–1991), in the 1940s, launched a new wave of interest in Yogic religions by presenting the practice of yoga as a healthy form of exercise. Then in 1961, Hittleman managed to persuade a television producer in Los Angeles to make a program about the health benefits of yoga, introducing yoga to millions of Americans. In his 1969 best-selling book *Guide to Yoga Meditation*, Hittleman confesses that his stress on yoga as a healthy exercise was actually a hook to lead America to embrace Hinduism. As a result, the idea that yoga was a healthy form of exercise got ordinary Americans interested in Hinduism.[17]

What Hittleman did not say was that the promotion of Hinduism using physical exercises was first developed by Swami Vivekananda in the late nineteenth century. Like Hittleman after him, Vivekananda recognized that Westerners, with the exception of a few philosophers, had little interest in Hindu religious beliefs and practices. He concluded that attempts by people like his mentor Ramakrishna (1836–1886) to spread Hindu beliefs to the West were unlikely to succeed.

In May 1897 Vivekananda founded the Ramakrishna Mission to promote the monistic philosophy of Ramakrishna by teaching what he claimed were healthy exercises that were an ancient form of spirituality he called yoga. For both Vivekananda and Hittleman, the ploy worked. Westerners flocked to learn yoga exercises wrapped in Hindu terminology.

The irony is that the exercises introduced to the West as ancient forms of Indian spirituality were anything but that, yet no one recognized this until American scholar and yoga practitioner Mark Singleton began to explore the history of modern yoga. What Singleton reveals in his fascinating *Yoga Body: The Origins of Modern Posture Practice*, published in 2010, is that what we know today as "yoga exercises" originated as a form of gymnastic exercise taught by the YMCA and popularized in Europe, especially Scandinavia.[18] It was the genius of Vivekananda, and after him Hittleman, to link these exercises to Indian spirituality. Yet, in reality, there is no connection between the practice of the exercises and Indian religious beliefs.

Conclusion

What is important for Christians to realize is that the Yogic tradition relies more on oral traditions transmitted and created by gurus, who are seen as living gods, than do Abramic religions that are firmly rooted in unchangeable Scriptures. As a result, although there are scriptures, like the Vedas, Upanishads, and numerous lesser texts, the guru can interpret them far more freely based on his own spiritual experiences and insights than members of Abramic faiths can interpret their own Scriptures. With this in mind, we now turn to the two major branches of the Yogic tradition, Buddhism and Hinduism.

chapter six

The Way of the Buddha

Introduction

World religions textbooks usually discuss the Hindu tradition before talking about Buddhism. This is based on the common dating of Buddhist and Hindu texts and the assumption that Buddhism was a reform movement within the Hindu tradition. As will be seen in the next chapter, arriving at this conclusion is not as straightforward as it may seem.

Many Buddhists believe the Buddhist tradition predates the Hindu tradition or, at the very least, is just as old. This is because Buddhist inscriptions in India pre-date Hindu inscriptions by hundreds of years. Extant Buddhist texts, meaning existing manuscripts found in museums and private collections, are far older than the earliest extant Hindu texts. As a result, there appears to be little physical evidence supporting the claim that something like what we know as Hinduism existed before Buddhism.

While it is here assumed that Buddhism is a separate religious tradition from the Hindu tradition, the two may have common roots. Either way, to fully appreciate the Buddhist tradition, we need to recover its originality and recognize that it is at least as old as the Hindu tradition.

The Buddhist Story

The first thing to recognize about Buddhism is that although Buddha is acknowledged as its founder, he is usually not seen as the first to embrace the essential ideas of his religion. His achievement was to make these ideas available to a wider audience than any other teacher had done, although throughout history many Buddha figures had appeared to bring the message to humanity.

According to Buddhist tradition, the figure we know as the Buddha was born as a prince around 150 miles from Benares on the border between India and modern Nepal. There he grew up and was married and had at least one son in what seemed like an idyllic situation where he lived in great luxury. Then one day, when he was around thirty years old, something dramatic changed his life. There are various slightly different accounts of this event. In sum, Prince Siddhartha, as he was known, went out of his palace one day and, in quick succession, met a young child full of energy and joy, followed by an old and decrepit man in great pain. Then he met a younger man who was very sick and clearly approaching the point of death. Finally, he met a funeral procession carrying a decaying corpse. The rapid sequence of events came as a surprise and deeply shocked him.

After reflecting on these encounters, Siddhartha made the hard decision to totally change his life. He abandoned his family and went in search of spiritual truth. This act of wrenching himself free from his family and past life is known as the "Great Renunciation." He wandered India for about six years. He visited numerous spiritual teachers and holy men and practiced all sorts of meditation and forms of spirituality. Yet he found no peace. He became a hermit, studied philosophy, and practiced eating only six grains of rice a day. When all of this failed to enlighten him, he tried excessive indulgence and drinking himself into stupors. None of these brought satisfaction and he was in despair.

At the end of his tether, Siddhartha sat under a fig tree, which was later given the name *bohdi tree*, or tree of wisdom and enlightenment. Here, he fought a terrifying battle with Mara, a godlike being who blinds humans to the reality of this world of illusion. After this struggle and without the aid of religious teachers or devotions, he experienced enlightenment and became the Buddha.

His grim experience resolved all his questions and gave him understanding into the nature of existence. All life, he realized, is suffering, meaning not simply that life involves suffering but that being in its very essence is suffering. Nothing exists that is not part of suffering. Suffering is the essence of all things in this earthly existence.

The only solution to the anguish of life, he realized, comes not from asceticism or hedonism, but by embracing what he called "the middle way." Buddhists believe that after the enlightenment of the Buddha, the heavens shook, stars deviated from their courses, and the whole cosmos was deeply affected. Blossoms became fruits, fruits ripened on trees, and the sky shone unseen glory. A pivotal event in human history had taken place.

Following his enlightenment, the Buddha meditated on the truths he had discovered before deciding to share them with others. He began to make disciples, and Buddhism was born. As his followers grew in number, the Buddha began to send out what in Christian terms would be called evangelists, or traveling preachers, who spread throughout India and eventually all of Asia. The Buddha's early followers were men, and it seems he had no initial intention of including women in his movement. Then one day his cousin Ananda pleaded for the inclusion of women, and the Buddha founded an order of nuns.

Exactly when these events took place is unknown, but the death of the Buddha is often dated around 483 BC. Following his death, over the next few centuries, a series of Great Councils were held by monks, and eventually two great Buddhist movements developed.

These were the Mahayana, or Great Vehicle, which was more inclusive of the laity, and the Theravada, or Lesser Vehicle, which was essentially monastic. Theravadan Buddhism spread from India to Sri Lanka and throughout Southeast Asia, while Mahayanan Buddhism spread from India into Tibet and Korea. From Korea it moved into China and Japan, where it took on local color and developed into new forms of what would become a world religion.

Buddhism's Golden Age

According to tradition, the golden age of Buddhism began in the third century BC and lasted to around the seventh century AD. The era began with the conversion of King Asoka (d. 232 BC), grandson of Chandragupta, the founder of the Indian Maurya Dynasty. This dynasty lasted from around 322 BC to 187 BC, eventually controlling a vast area of the Indian subcontinent that today would include large parts of Afghanistan, India, and Pakistan.

The rapid expansion of Buddhism began with the conversion of King Asoka, who had consolidated the Maurya Dynasty by defeating its enemies and extending his rule over most of the Indian subcontinent. Following his last major battle, which led to the deaths of between 100,000 and 200,000 people, Asoka is reported to have been disgusted by the destruction, and then he encountered holy men who probably were Buddhist priests.

This encounter led him to change his ways and become a peaceful king who, if he did not convert to Buddhism as tradition tells us, certainly created the conditions for it to flourish throughout India. Here the history is vague. It is unclear whether Asoka actually converted following a major battle, but what is certain is that he laid the foundation for the spread of Buddhism, and by the end of his life had become a believer. Following the reign of Asoka, his children promoted Buddhism and it experienced a golden age.

The map below shows the spread of Buddhism from around 300

BC to 1400 AD. Note the way Buddhism spread across India before finally dying out in the land of its birth between the twelfth and fourteenth centuries. When Buddhism first entered China, the Han dynasty was firmly in control of a vast area stretching from Turkistan to Korea to Vietnam and to the Gobi Desert. Officially the Han dynasty was committed to Confucianism as a way of life that emphasized filial piety, maintenance of social rights, and an explicit moral code with clearly defined social rules, yet over time China became a center of Buddhism.

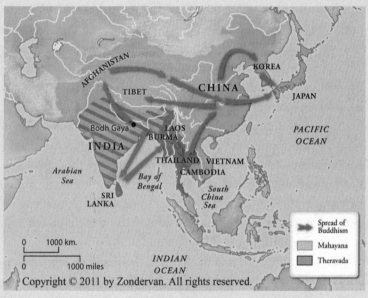

Map showing the spread of Buddhism during its golden age.

Around 65 AD, Emperor Ming (reigned 58–76 AD) is said to have had a vision of the Buddha. As a result, he permitted the building of the Whitehorse Temple. Within a hundred years, Buddhist worship and practices were common at the imperial court.

In 399 AD the Buddhist monk Fa-Hsien made a historic journey to India where he gathered source materials about the life and teachings of the Buddha. This journey encouraged a series of pilgrimages to India by Chinese Buddhists who sought to discover more about the founder of their religion. In addition to visiting India, Fa-Hsien visited all the major Buddhist pilgrimage sites throughout the subcontinent and even went to Sri Lanka. He returned to China in 414, laden with priceless Buddhist manuscripts.

Around the same time, an Indian Buddhist monk, Kumarajiva, was kidnapped by Chinese pirates and sold into slavery in the provincial capital of Ch'ang-an. There he eventually gathered around him 300 Chinese scholars and supervised the translation of numerous Mahayanan sutras into Chinese. By the end of the late fourth century AD, most of northern China was converted to Buddhism. Things changed in 446 AD when one of the northern Chinese rulers apostatized and initiated a period of savage persecution. Eventually he was overthrown, and Buddhism was restored by his successors as a religion of the people.

Another period of vicious persecution against Buddhists occurred during the reign of Emperor Wu, who drove over a million monks and nuns from their temples, forcing them to become laypeople. Much like Henry the VIII and his supporters in Reformation England, the imperial family, local aristocrats, and opportunist individuals benefited from these persecutions by seizing temple lands and enriching themselves on the accumulated treasures of Buddhist communities.

This period of persecution came to an end when Emperor Wen founded a new dynasty in 581 AD. Identifying himself as a disciple of the Buddha, he ushered in an era of Buddhist art and scholarship in China. Like the earlier Indian emperor Asoka, he supported missionary efforts and sought to spread Buddhism far beyond the borders of his realm. In particular he sought to convert Koreans and Japanese to Buddhism. For the next 250 years, Buddhism spread throughout the regions bordering China without serious opposition. In 845 AD, a third wave of bitter persecution swept through China, and from then on, Chinese Buddhists experienced periods of growth and decline depending on the inclination of the ruling regime.

Buddhism fared well in Korea following its introduction in 372 AD, when it became the major religion of the country. After establishment of the fiercely pro-neo-Confucian Choson, or Yi, dynasty, Buddhism was savagely suppressed and marginalized in Korean society without further state support. Nevertheless, Korean Buddhism retained a strong undercurrent in the religiosity of the common people and preserved some of the most important collections of Buddhist scriptures.

Korean Buddhist civilization reached the height of its power between the twelfth and fourteenth centuries when Buddhism attracted the best of the aristocracy and ruling elite. A change of dynasty in 1392 led to the establishment of a strict neo-Confucian regime that excluded Buddhism from circles of power and persecuted it in varying degrees. Nevertheless, Buddhism continued to maintain support among the common people.

Buddhism was introduced to Japan from Korea in 552 AD with support of members of the Japanese nobility. Although periods of persecution and neglect followed, Japanese Buddhists in general fared much better than their Korean neighbors up until the fifteenth century, leading to development of a number of important schools of Buddhist thought and practice. The best known of the schools is, of course, Zen. Buddhism's fortunes declined from the fifteenth century on and went into sharp decline during the Tokugawa period (1603–1867), when neo-Confucianism became the dominant philosophy, and militant Shinto led to sporadic persecutions of Buddhists. By the late nineteenth century, it appeared that Buddhism would die out in Japan, but a revival occurred that continued throughout the twentieth century to the present.

The situation in India was initially one of remarkable success that saw the flowering of Buddhist culture throughout most of the subcontinent, particularly in the north. All this came to an end around 900 AD when large areas of northern India were overrun by Muslim invaders. Suddenly, Chinese and Tibetan Buddhism was cut off from the source of Buddhist scholarship and piety as Muslims massacred thousands of priests, destroyed ancient Buddhist temples, and annihilated centers of Buddhist learning. From the Buddhist viewpoint, these massacres were nothing less than a holocaust.

A fate similar to the one that struck northern India occurred almost simultaneously in the area we know today as Afghanistan and affected numerous smaller kingdoms along the Silk Route. Between 700 and 900 AD, one after another of the Buddhist kingdoms of Central Asia fell to invading Arabs who established Islamic states. Within a couple of centuries, the heartland of Buddhism became an area where Islam flourished. Only in small isolated pockets, in secluded valleys and remote regions, could an emaciated form of Buddhism survive, cut off from the roots of its tradition until the twentieth century.

Buddhist Texts and Scriptures

Unlike other religious traditions, Buddhism has a vast number of scriptures. Traditionally these are divided into two groups known as the Dharma, or Sutras, and the Vinaya. The Dharma consists of doctrinal texts while the Vinaya contains the rules of monastic discipline. Later, a third division of scripture was added, the Abhidharma, which aimed at systematizing the contents of the Sutras.

A sutra is a text that was traditionally believed to have been spoken by the Buddha himself. All sutras begin with the words, "Thus have I heard that the Lord . . ." Here the speaker is assumed to be Ananda, the Buddha's cousin and favorite disciple. In actuality, many sutras were composed hundreds of years after the death of the Buddha.

One of the major divisions between the Hinayana, and later Theravada, tradition and that of the Mahayana revolves around the issue of which scriptures are to be accepted as authentic. The Theravadan position is that only those scriptures that were recited at the first council following the Buddha's death are to be accepted. The Mahayana, on the other hand, accept numerous scriptures as authentic. They do this on the basis of their doctrine of multiple Buddhas and their belief that the Buddha was simply the incarnation of the Buddha principle. Some Mahayana teachers also assert that many sutras composed after the death of the Buddha were spoken by him but stored in the netherworld, because they were too difficult for the people of his time to understand. Only when the time was ripe were they brought into our world by committed Buddhists.

The composition date of Buddhist scriptures is difficult to ascertain. Only a few can even be dated in terms of when they were discovered and where. Generally, modern scholars place the death of the Buddha around 483 BC; traditional views give a variety of dates from 852 to 252 BC. This is understandable in light of Buddhism's ahistorical orientation. What matters is the teaching, not how we got it.

For many centuries, Buddhist teachings were part of an oral tradition transmitted from teacher to pupil or pupils. Later these teachings were written down. The earliest written works we possess date from around the second century AD, although there are inscriptions from the time of Asoka. The earliest scriptures were likely written between two hundred and three hundred years after the death of the Buddha and possibly longer. The earliest existing copies come from around the third century AD, about seven hundred years after the death of the Buddha.

One of the earliest collections of Buddhist scriptures considered to be authentic within the Theravadan tradition is known as the Pali Canon. This collection of works was composed in Sri Lanka in the Pali language. It consists of works grouped together under three headings to form three distinct sections. Together they are known as the Tripitaka. In Pali, these are referred to as *pitakas*, or baskets. The three baskets are those of discipline pertaining to monastic life, sermons that report the teachings of the Buddha, and metaphysical texts dealing with philosophical issues. The other major collection of this sort is the Chinese Tripitaka, which is generally broader in scope than its Pali counterpart. The oldest catalog of this Chinese collection can be dated to 518 AD when it was said to contain 2,113 works. Of these texts, only 276 still exist.

Another major collection of Buddhist texts is the Tibetan *Kanjur* and *Tanjur*. The *Kanjur* contains somewhere between 100 and 108 distinct volumes, while the *Tanjur* consists of somewhere between 209 and 225 volumes. In addition to these works, numerous other scriptures exist based on translations from Sanskrit texts. These include a collection of stories about the birth of the Buddha known as the *Jataka*. Altogether thousands of Buddhist manuscripts, many of which remain untranslated into English, still exist. Many of these were found during the twentieth century in remote areas of central Asia, where they had been carefully buried to protect them from invaders and where the dry climate could preserve them for hundreds of years.

What Buddhists Believe

Buddhist beliefs in two areas present immediate problems for the outside observer, particularly for a Christian. These areas are God and human nature.

Many years ago, my wife was interrogated by South African security police shortly after she interviewed an African religious leader. When she learned that the African "prophet" whom she interviewed the previous day had been taken into custody, she exclaimed in horror, "Oh! My God!" to which the South African police officer wryly commented, "God has nothing to do with it."

In many ways the South African policeman's answer was profoundly Buddhist. Buddhists do not deny the existence of God or, for that matter, the existence of gods. What they argue, and as far as we can tell what the Buddha taught, is that God or the gods have nothing to say about humans' ultimate fate. Only the Buddha has shown the way beyond this realm of existence.

The unimportance of God to the ultimate fate of humans is linked to the Buddhist view of human nature. Most of us are used to thinking of ourselves as individual persons, possessing something we all call "the self." Whether this self is a living soul or simply a being who has some sort of individualized existence, it does not matter. For the Buddhist, the self does not exist.

At least for most Buddhists there is no such thing as "the person," although in the first period of Buddhist history, an important school of Indian Buddhism was known as the Personalists. Even these Buddhists, though they believed it possible to talk about a person, ultimately denied the existence of a self. They argued on the basis of Buddhist philosophy, over and above the sense impressions that create our awareness of the world, that there is something that can meaningfully be called "a person." However, a person was not to be thought of as permanent or as anything more than a momentary surge of consciousness. They argued that the person was real while the self was not. Although influential at one time, the school was vanquished after centuries of philosophical argument often involving public debates where sometimes the losers lost their lives. It eventually disappeared.

For the vast majority of Buddhists, there is neither a self nor a person. All that exists in terms of the human being is a series of sense impressions that can be analyzed with great precision. The sense impressions are made up of the skandhas, or groupings, and a part of an impersonal dharma.

In the Buddhist scheme, there are three jewels, or treasures, to which each individual must cling if they are to attain enlightenment.

The first jewel is a Buddha himself. Contrary to some popular West-ern interpretations and even some ancient developments to Bud-dhism, such as certain branches of Zen, Buddha is absolutely essential to Buddhist teachings because it is a Buddha who guarantees truth.

Equally confusing for many Westerners is the fact that like the term "Christ," the term "Buddha" is not a personal name but a title, meaning "enlightened one." Enlightenment in this case refers to someone who is totally free from any spiritual or material forces that hinder his or her appreciation of the truth of reality itself, the dharma, and the teachings of the Buddha. Yet within Buddhism, the Buddha is far more than simply a historical human being. The Buddha is also the being that is identified with the essence of what is called "Buddha nature," or "the Tathagata," whose reality is also referred to as "the dharma body of the Buddha." In other words, there is a super-mundane, or perhaps we should say supernatural, aspect to the Buddha. Within early Buddhism as we know it, people spoke about seven Buddhas, of which the historical Buddha was the last. Each of these Buddhas was said to have appeared on earth during a period of great need with the express intent of preaching the dharma to all "sentient beings" and thus restoring a balance to the universe.

This view of the Buddha, as a manifestation of the principal Buddhahood that eventually grew from seven Buddhas to twenty-four Buddhas, and in some traditions to many more, gave way to the idea of the Buddha body. It came to be believed that even when he was on earth, over and above the physical appearance of the Bud-dha's body was an ethereal, supernatural body that was only visible to highly spiritual people. This spiritual body of the Buddha is said to be sixteen feet high and contain thirty-two marks of a superman. These marks include wheels engraved on his feet, webbed fingers, and what Christians would call a halo around his head. The full development of this doctrine of the Buddha, his various manifesta-tions, and his supernatural body took centuries. By the end of the first millennium of Buddhism, all these beliefs appear to have been firmly in place. Thus, the Buddha was seen as not just a man, nor as a god, but as an extraordinary being who brings enlightenment to other sentient beings.

Alongside the development of doctrines about the Buddha there developed new understandings of the dharma, the second jewel of Buddhism. The dharma was said to protect, transmit, and maintain the truth of Buddhism. So important was the dharma within the Buddhist community that in Asia, Buddhists were not known as Buddhists but rather as followers of the dharma. This dharma is the impersonal spiritual reality upon which everything is based. Grasping the true extent of the dharma is like trying to drink all the water as it flows from a tap or a mountain stream.

There are various aspects to dharma in Buddhism. First, the dharma represents, or comprises, the whole of reality. It is the only true reality in contrast to the world of illusion in which we all live. Second, the dharma refers to the Buddha's teachings, his doctrines, the sutras, and the truth of his message. It is, in other words, the sum total of Buddhist teaching. Third, the dharma can be seen to take form in the action of human beings, and in that sense, it is similar to the Christian concept of righteousness, or the ancient Roman concepts of virtue and *gravitas*, which implies a serious attitude toward life.

Within Buddhist writings there are frequent references not simply to the dharma, but also to dharmas. This plural usage signifies the basic elements of consciousness or whatever ties experienced reality together. By way of contrast, the dharmas, which should not be confused with "the dharma," are like atoms to the physicist. Within Buddhism there are many lists of dharmas. For example, the five skandhas that make up the basic elements of human personality are dharmas. These are corporality, feelings, perceptions, volition, and consciousness. Identifying the dharmas and understanding the workings of consciousness are essential to Buddhist meditation.

It is only in this way that the Buddhist comes to see the non-reality of everything we consider reality.

The last of the three jewels is the Sangha, or Buddhist community, which preserves the teachings of the Buddha, the lifestyle of his followers, and the practices of meditation, which are only possible within a supportive community. Although many so-called Western Buddhists play down the importance of the Sangha, it is nevertheless vital for authentic Buddhism.

Buddhism is both a highly philosophical and an experiential religious system. Central to its practices and beliefs are the four Noble Truths. The first Noble Truth is the truth of dukkha, or impermanence, which is often rendered as suffering, but in fact they are separate ideas with impermanence being the cause of suffering. What it means is that nothing in life is lasting; everything is in a constant state of flux. Even if you are happy today, you may be sacked tomorrow. If you are young today, you will be old tomorrow. Everything changes. The flowers bloom, and then they wither away. This is the essence of life. There is no permanence. There is no lasting satisfaction. There is only eternal change and impermanence. Hence, all life is described as suffering.

The second Noble Truth is the cause of the suffering created by impermanence. According to Buddhist thought, impermanence and suffering are caused by our craving or thirst for existence. In other words, our consciousness emerges from constant activities that are bound to the totality of all things that are in constant motion. This consciousness, which results from individual events, creates the illusion that an individual person, or self, actually exists, when in reality all that exists is a constant motion of impermanent sense impressions.

The third Noble Truth is that the cause of this impermanence or suffering can be eliminated. There is a way that leads to the annihilation of consciousness. There is a way that leads to the cessation of all activity. This is the way that the Buddha has shown to his followers.

The fourth Noble Truth is that way, known as the Noble Eightfold Path. This path consists of eight levels, or steps, that lead the individual consciousness to enlightenment. The full path has three basic elements. These are trust in the teachings of the Buddha, the living of an ethical and pure life, and the correct way to meditate and thus bring the mind to total control. The first steps on the path deal with the essence of trust. They are right belief and right attitude. Without knowing what is true and without having a receptive attitude, one can never follow the path.

The next three steps deal with the way we live. They are right speech, right actions, and right livelihood. The Buddhist must constantly be aware of what they say because their words reflect their thoughts. Since thoughts lead to action, and actions reflect thoughts, then how a Buddhist behaves is essential to correct living. Finally, how a person makes their living will affect their speech and actions. For example, if a person works in a slaughterhouse killing animals, their thoughts and actions lead them away from the truth of Buddhism. As a Buddhist, such work cannot be done.

The final three steps are concerned with the control of the mind through meditation, or yoga. These steps are right effort, right awareness, and right meditation. To act rightly, one must always struggle to do what is good in terms of Buddhist teaching about right and wrong. Right awareness, or contemplation, means that one must learn to control the mind so that emotions and the concerns of life do not affect one's inner being. Thus, neither joy nor sorrow, heat nor cold, wealth nor poverty, nor any other transitory state should affect the inner thoughts of the true Buddhist. Finally, there is right meditation, contemplation, or perhaps we should say the right practice of Buddhist yoga. Only when all the other stages of the eightfold pattern have been followed is it possible to bring the mind totally under the control of the will. Only when all is still does the possibility exist of attaining enlightenment. This possibility is the ultimate goal of Buddhism.

Buddhist Enlightenment

So what is enlightenment exactly? Buddhists call it nirvana and have great difficulty explaining what it is. Perhaps the best explanations come from the Buddhist sutras that go back to the Buddha himself. According to these traditions, to the question "What is nirvana?" the Buddha answered by asking, "Where does the flame go when you blow out a candle?" What he meant by this was that nirvana is the unknown, the unconditioned, experienced enlightenment. If this makes no sense to the reader, it is because nirvana is beyond human comprehension.

Edward Conze begins his book *Buddhism: Its Essence and Development* by saying Buddhism attracts only people who are completely disillusioned with the world. To most Westerners, Conze's view of the human condition seems pessimistic, but practitioners of Buddhism would disagree. Buddhism portrays a very different form of salvation than do the Abramic religions. The latter place value on human personality and emphasize the salvation of the individual, while Yogic religions speak of salvation *away from* individuality. As Ninian Smart has written, Yogic thinking, upon which Buddhism is based, holds that

> men and other living beings are continually being reborn. With death, the individual is reborn in a different form. This everlasting recurrence of births and deaths can only be stopped by transcending it, by attaining a liberation into a transcendental sphere where the self is freed from mental and bodily encumbrances. Typically, this is achieved by the practice of austerity and yoga: self-denial and self-discipline are means of destroying that which leads to rebirth and Karma.[1]

Buddhist ideas of rebirth are logically related to belief in karma, but need to be differentiated from Hindu views. Buddhists deny the existence of the soul, arguing that the continuation of sense impressions at the point of death deludes those who suffer near-death experiences into thinking that they have an essence or soul. Buddhists postulate reincarnation rather than transmigration of the soul. They define rebirth through transmigration as the continuation of sense impressions, not the movement of the soul from one body to another.

Buddhist Piety

Buddhist piety centers on practices of meditation that were originally designed for monks. These practices aim at bringing the mind under control so that the mediator recognizes the true nature of reality and is able to escape from it. Yet talk about meditation can be somewhat misleading. What in English we call meditation covers three different ideas within Buddhism. First, there is the idea of mindfulness, which is the first stage in meditation. Traditionally, this is seen as a quieting of the mind or the calming down of thought. Mindfulness in turn leads to both wisdom and ultimately trance.

Second, there is the idea of concentration, which draws upon the Buddhist belief that our mind has two levels. The first level is that of ordinary consciousness. It is the surface level of the mind. Beneath this is a deeper level that is calm. Few people are aware of, or able to reach, this deeper level. Most people live in a state of constant turmoil.

Finally, there is the idea of wisdom, which in Buddhism is the highest of all values. For the Buddhist, the idea of wisdom is quite specific. The great Ceylonese Buddhist scholar Buddhaghosa (fifth century AD) defined it as "whatever penetrates into the Dharmas destroying all the illusions of darkness which distort our understanding the Dharma."[2] It may be said that wisdom concerns the meaning of life, our daily conduct, and the essence of reality.

The Buddhist Calendar

Because Buddhism has taken root in various cultures and societies, there is no one Buddhist calendar like the Christian year. Instead we have various Buddhist calendars adapted to different countries and traditions. In attempting to understand Buddhist festivals, it is important to recognize that, as in Jewish and other traditions, Buddhists work with the lunar calendar. The Buddhist year begins with the full moon that marks the day the Buddha is said to have been born.

Most Buddhists celebrate two major festivals. In the Therevadan tradition, the first festival is known as Wesakh, which celebrates the birth, death, and enlightenment of the Buddha on the first full moon of the second lunar month. During this festival, people wear white gowns, raise flags, and light lanterns. They also attach money to branches known as money trees. The second festival is Kathina, which is a time to celebrate the poor, give gifts, and endow monks with new robes. Other festivals, such as a celebration of the Chinese New Year, are often incorporated into Buddhist celebrations.

Buddhist Devotions

Most Buddhists maintain a small shrine in their homes to aid them in meditation. In such a shrine there will be at least one statue of the Buddha and very often candles or a low light. There may also be other decorations depicting the Buddha or Buddhist scriptures. Buddhists also use a rosary, a string of beads, usually 118 in number, to aid them in their meditations.

Buddhists wear ordinary clothes while attending communal celebrations, which Christians tend to describe as worship. Of course, since God and the gods are essentially unimportant for Buddhism, it is somewhat misleading to speak about Buddhist worship. Perhaps a more accurate term is communal meditation or the veneration of the Buddha. When entering a Buddhist temple, which in North America and Europe is sometimes called a Buddhist church, shoes are removed and very often participants sit cross-legged on the floor. Many services are similar to those found in a church.

Looking Ahead

With this basic outline of Buddhism in mind, we will now assess Buddhism as a religion to live by. Can a person accept Buddhism and live a consistent life? What should a Christian think about Buddhism?

chapter seven

The Nothingness of Buddhism

Introduction

When I studied Buddhism at Lancaster University in England, we were fortunate enough to have Edward Conze (1904–1979) as our teacher after he had been refused reentry to the United States on the grounds that in the 1920s and 1930s he had been an active Communist. What was overlooked in this decision was the reason Conze, who had embraced Buddhism as a teenager, became a Communist.

According to him, and I believe he was telling the truth, it was because as a graduate student he was faced with the choice of either becoming a Nazi or joining the Communist Party, which he saw as the most efficient opposition group. So he chose Communism and bought into many Marxist ideas. As a result, he became an important organizer of anti-Nazi activities in Bonn and Hamburg.

Fortuitously, as he admitted himself, he had the good fortune, or as he said "karma," to have been born in London where his father was a German diplomat. Technically, he was a British citizen. This fact saved his life because after the Nazis came to power in 1933, most of his Communist colleagues were arrested and brutally beaten before many were killed. In his case, the SS paid him and his Jewish wife a visit to inform them that the government did not want to upset the British. Reluctant to arrest him, they gave him three days to leave Germany and claim his British citizenship. He took their advice.

Once in Britain, Conze abandoned all interest in politics and concentrated on his Buddhism. When war broke out, it was decided that his eyesight was too poor to allow him to join the army, and he spent the war years offering courses to civilians and the army. After the war, he moved to America, which he really loved, to become an itinerant scholar. Then, after a summer visit to his second wife's family in Britain, he was refused reentry to America on the grounds that he had been a Communist.

As a result, I was fortunate enough to have him as a teacher and to get to know him a little. By that time there was no hint of Marxism in his teaching. In fact, he despised the young radical "Marxist" scholars who were beginning to dominate British academic life. After a few years and a legal challenge, the restriction was lifted, and he was able to return to America once more. What he never explained, which is discussed in more detail later in this chapter, is why as a Buddhist he chose Buddhism over Marxism.

Misunderstanding Buddhism

Conze was a great teacher who began his course by outlining the history of Western Buddhism and denouncing various interpretations of Buddhism that were popular at the time. In doing so, he drew attention to the impact of British East India Company scholars and their successors who he claimed created Buddhism in their own image as a form of religious rationalism.

One of the key figures in this development was Sir Edwin Arnold (1832–1904), a liberal Christian and promoter of British Imperialism. His book-length poem *The Light of Asia* (1879) presented his understanding of the life of the Buddha as a supremely rational individual working for the good of humankind. It became an instant best seller in Britain and America before being translated into numerous other European languages. The Buddha is presented as a thinking individual whose beliefs contain none of the absurdities of other religions such as a belief in miracles or the supernatural.

Conze spurned this type of interpretation, pointing out that it violated the entire Buddhist tradition and classic texts by ignoring the role of such things as astrology, the demonic, miracles, and prophecies. As a practicing Buddhist, Conze had a firm belief in astrology and magic.

For example, before beginning his courses, which were usually small seminars of about ten students, Conze asked everyone present to provide him with their date of birth. He dismissed the class, telling us to go for coffee to get to know one another while he checked our horoscopes. When we met again two days later he had decided, on the basis of our horoscopes, whether he would allow us to remain in the class. Everyone in my class passed the test, but some students in other classes were politely told to withdraw. Today I doubt that any university would allow this, but it did bring home the importance of the supernatural in Buddhism to students who thought it was a purely rational religion.

Conze insisted that the supernatural was very much a part of daily life. At the time, this was a revolutionary way of teaching about Buddhism because he insisted that unless one grasps the importance of the supernatural in Buddhism, it is impossible to understand Buddhist teachings and practices. Today most, if not all, scholars agree with the main points of Conze's criticisms of earlier Western views of Buddhism that reduced this ancient religion to a form of rationalistic humanism, which it is not.

Developing a Christian Response to Buddhism

One of the best ways to approach Buddhism and practicing Buddhists is found in Tucker N. Callaway's *Zen Way: Jesus Way*.[1] In this fascinating work, Callaway, a Southern Baptist missionary in Japan, explains how he studied Zen Buddhism under the guidance of Zen Master Daisetz T. Suzuki (1870–1966). After his missionary career, his intensive study, and his teaching of world religions in Japan for thirty years, he wrote his book in which he argues that Christianity and Zen Buddhism are both internally consistent religious worldviews that can be embraced in good faith by anyone who takes the time to study them.

He nevertheless argues that one must choose, because while both religions are consistent and satisfying in their own way, they are completely incompatible. One can be a Buddhist or a Christian but not both, because they begin from totally different premises that lead to very different conclusions about the nature of life.

Edward Conze would have agreed with Callaway on this issue. He repeatedly brought home to his students that Buddhism is totally other. That is, it denies everything we take for granted. As a system, Buddhism denies everything ordinary people take for granted by starting with its doctrine of no-self. If there really is no-self, then all we know is an illusion and things like love are a mirage.

Callaway argues that anyone can accept this worldview provided they are able to live with the consequences. This is surely a starting point for anyone who tries to communicate Christianity to a Buddhist, because what most Buddhists seem to do is live a philosophically inconsistent life. The fact is that most Buddhists love their wives and children, and many have a real loving concern for others. But all of these beings are really an illusion, creating a problem for Buddhists who take their beliefs seriously.

We have already seen this in Conze's own reaction to the Nazis. If no person exists, why bother about the welfare of others? Why be concerned about Jews and others when in reality they have no essence? Conze never satisfactorily explained why, as a Buddhist, he was opposed to the Nazis. Why did he find them morally objectionable? Of course, we can all agree that he was right to do so. But why?

Another example of his inconsistency is that in explaining the nonexistence of the individual, Conze was clear that popular ideas about love were an illusion as were Christian teachings on the subject. One cannot love an impression that has no reality. If there is no person, there is nothing to love. In Buddhist thought, there is no place for love because one can love only a living being, be it a person or animal. Once we recognize that there is no actual being, then there is nothing to love. Consequently, "love is one of the most unsatisfactory and ambiguous terms."[2]

Conze once told his classes that "love is a mirage and sex is just like scratching an itch." The problem with this argument is that his wife, Muriel, who lived with him in a small apartment on the Lancaster University campus and was someone we saw, really seemed attached to him. She gave the impression of loving him very deeply. In return he appeared to love her and really care about her as a person. Even though he argued that sex was as irrelevant as an itch and had a reputation for philandering, he and Muriel appeared to have a genuine personal relationship. But the possibility of such a relationship was something he consistently denied.

The problem here is that people all over the world and in every conceivable type of circumstance do love other people. Buddhism presents logical arguments that this is impossible, but the logic clashes with the experience of most people. Buddhists do love their husbands, wives, and families. People love and see others as persons, not abstract conglomerations of atoms bouncing around an endless universe. At this point Buddhism seems to fail a crucial test of truth that was proposed by Edward John Carnell (1919–1967) in his now classic work *An Introduction to Christian Apologetics*.[3]

Carnell, one of the founders of Fuller Theological Seminary, argued that all religions and religious believers have to face two key tests related to systematic consistency. To rephrase his complex arguments, the first test was that of logical consistency: a belief system must conform to the rules of logic and present rational arguments.

The second test was that philosophical arguments must cohere with reality as we know it. Logic and experience go together to create a consistent whole and ought not to be separated.

We must carefully examine the arguments of any religious or philosophical system to ensure that they actually hold together in a coherent way. Then we need to ask if this coherence fits the facts of life. That is, do they make sense of our experiences?

When these tests are applied to Buddhism, there is no doubt that Buddhist beliefs are logically self-consistent, at least as far as most people's understanding of them goes. They provide what appears to be a remarkably logical interpretation of the world. The problem with these beliefs comes from the fact that they are not consistent with daily experience. In fact, Edward Conze begins his classic work *Buddhism: Its Essence and Development*[4] by stating that the central belief and practice of Buddhism is "the extinction of the belief in individuality," by which is meant all those things that cause a person to believe that they are in any sense a "self" or actual "person."[5]

Buddhism and War

Another problem with Buddhism is the way it was presented to the West as a religion of peace. Today Buddhism appeals to many people because it is seen as the only truly peaceful religion. This is a big problem for Christians because since the Enlightenment, Christianity has been presented as having a violent history "soaked in blood." Buddhism is said to be unique because it is genuinely peaceful. This perspective is part of a popular apologetic produced by theosophical Buddhists, such as Henry Steel Olcott (1832–1907), intended to make Buddhism more palatable to the West.

Until recently, the only way to answer this argument was by pointing to the actions of Buddhists in history and groups like the Japanese Samurai, who were a formidable military force. But few people know much about Asian history, and almost no one took any notice of such arguments.

Then Brian Victoria, a practicing Buddhist and ordained priest, published a series of articles on Zen[6] and the role of the famous Zen practitioner and advocate D. T. Suzuki. In them he pointed out that before World War II, Suzuki was a promotor of Zen as a military creed capable of creating and sustaining the Japanese Empire. In his subsequent book *Zen at War*[7] he exposed the involvement of Japanese Buddhists in World War II and the inbuilt martial aspects of the Buddhist tradition. Later, and quite independent of Victoria, scholars like Karla Poewe discovered links between Nazi Germany and various Buddhist and Hindu ideas.[8]

A different, yet somewhat related, Christian response to Buddhism is found in the work of Paul Williams. For more than thirty years, he was both one of the leading British converts to Buddhism and a highly respected scholar of Mahayana Buddhism. Then he shocked his colleagues and others by announcing his conversion to Christianity. The reasons he gave, documented in his book *The Unexpected Way*,[9] are very informative.

After studying Buddhism since his mid-teens, Williams became one of the world's top experts. Then, while teaching Buddhism in the Department of Theology and Religious Studies at the University of Bristol, he found himself working with a group of Christian scholars. Devout Christians, they took his ideas seriously and were willing to share their beliefs with him while listening to his reasons for embracing Buddhism. Over time their rational approach and informed presentation of Christianity led to his conversion.

Two things played a key role in this transformation. First, his study of Buddhist texts led him to the conclusion that despite all the rhetoric, there was no clear affirmation that salvation, in terms of release from the endless bonds of existence, was really possible. However hard one might try, one was faced with the prospect of an eternal cycle of rebirth with no hope of change. In other words, following the Buddhist way for eternity might make absolutely no difference at all. So what was the point?

Second, and more importantly, he became convinced that the resurrection of Jesus was a historical fact that demonstrated both the existence of God and the reality of his love for humans. For him, Buddhism failed to meet the twin criteria of truth and experience, while Christianity met these conditions.

What Williams's story shows is that if Christians are prepared to listen to Buddhists and others and enter into meaningful discussions where both parties share their faith in an honest and open way, then it is possible to convince someone even if they are a leading academic expert with a command of Buddhist history and philosophy. What is needed is patience, because conversions of this type take many years and a real basis of friendship where people are willing to drop their defenses and discuss their beliefs and experiences in an open and honest manner.

All of this brings us back to the importance of the person. Christianity is unique in the religious marketplace in that it places a unique value on each individual because God loves all people. It is crucial for individuals and church communities to demonstrate the truth of their faith through living it in ways that impact the lives of others for good. But let there be no mistake, this is not an easy task. It is a task that will take a lifetime.

chapter eight

The Bewildering Complexity of Hinduism

Introduction

Of all the world religions, Hinduism, or as many people prefer to say the Hindu tradition, is probably the most difficult to explain and write about. This is because it offers believers such a wide range of options. Someone who is both a believing and practicing Hindu can legitimately claim to be an atheist, a monotheist, a polytheist, or remain agnostic. In other words, the next Hindu you meet may embrace a wide range of beliefs and practices that are totally different from the beliefs and practices of the last Hindu you talked to, and this can be very confusing.

There are many reasons for this tolerance of a very fluid system of beliefs and practices. The main one is that traditionally only someone born of Hindu parents and living in what is probably best described as the Indian subcontinent, its extensions into parts of Myanmar, and nearby countries was considered a Hindu. Whatever they believed didn't alter their birthright as a Hindu, leading to a toleration of different beliefs. Conversion to Hinduism was impossible. With the Hindu renaissance of the early nineteenth century, things began to change, and now many, but certainly not all, Hindus allow for the inclusion of converts into the Hindu community.

In thinking about and writing about the beliefs and practices of Hindus, one has to be very careful and will almost certainly say things that some Hindus will argue are wrong. To an extent, this happens with most religions, but in the Hindu case, it is far easier to miss things. With this in mind, we will try to outline the main tenets of the Hindu tradition before offering a Christian commentary on it in the next chapter.

The Literature of the Hindu Tradition

The Hindu tradition is rooted in a collection of writings known as the Vedas. The meaning of *veda* is knowledge, and there are four main collections of sacred scriptures known as the Vedas. These are the *Rig Veda*, the *Sama Veda*, the *Yajur Veda*, and the *Atharva Veda*. Together they form the Vedic corpus. Each Veda in turn contains different types of text.

Until recently, the most problematic of the Vedas for European scholarship and sophisticated Hindus was the *Atharva Veda*. This is because it consists of magical spells, healing remedies, love potions, curses, and similar incantations. These contradicted the pro-Hindu propaganda that many early European scholars, the Theosophists, and people like Swami Vivekananda tried to project of a religion that was more in tune with modern science than Christianity. To the pioneers of Hindu studies in the West and scholars like Oxford professor Max Müller, this Veda appeared to be particularly "primitive" and lacking in spirituality. Seen from today's perspective, it is similar to many so-called New Age texts and is generally accepted for what it is by recent Western scholarship.

For Hindus, the *Vedas* are both sacred and the basis of all Indian philosophical thought. Unlike the Bible, the *Vedas* are rarely read or studied by ordinary Hindus and are reserved for ritual specialists and students in Western countries. The sounds associated with the various *Vedas* and their repetition are far more important to Hindus than the study of the Vedas because reciting the Vedas is believed to have cosmic significance. As a result, only a few *Vedic* hymns are well known and in common use in major rituals and private devotions, while most remain virtually unknown to the average Hindu.

Within the Hindu tradition, the Brahmins are an exclusive class, or caste, whose duty it is to preserve the purity of the *Vedas* and repeat them from memory on ritual occasions. As a group, the Brahmins are the custodians of the Hindu religious tradition and its sacred texts. This reliance upon memory by the Brahmins allows Hindus to claim that the Vedas are thousands of years old and go back to at least 2500 BC; however, the very earliest surviving texts come from the sixteenth century AD.

The Vedas are considered by most Hindus to be a revelation and therefore authoritative. Exactly what is meant by revelation in the Hindu tradition is a matter of dispute. Some Hindu philosophical schools see the Vedas as supernatural revelations. Others see them as inspired texts with a status similar to the Bible. The most common understanding of the *Vedas* in the West is that of the Vedanta school of thought, which is the dominant school of Indian philosophy today. For its members, the Vedas are eternal texts without human authorship. They believe that the Vedas were revealed to humankind by men who simply recited divine revelations.

In many ways this Vedantic understanding mirrors the Muslim understanding of revelation, or *wahy*, which claims that Muhammad recited the Qur'an as he received it directly from God. Many people in the Hindu tradition hold a belief similar to the Muslim view of revelation, which allows no room for human authorship. In other words, there are no human sources for these scriptures, which means they cannot be examined critically by historians.

Interpretation of the Vedas is at least as varied as that of interpretations of the Bible, unlike in classical Islam where there are several clearly defined schools of interpretation. Through the centuries, numerous modes of interpreting the texts and expounding the meanings of the *Vedas* emerged. These interpretations originated in the great epic poems of the *Ramayana* and the *Mahabharata,* which are sometimes called the fifth *Veda.*

Interpretations are also found in texts known as the *Puranas* and works that are attributed to the legendary figure of Bharata, who is said to have composed his famous *Natya sastra* sometime around 300 AD. In fact, the earliest fragmentary form of this major text dates from the fifth century AD. Its exact date is uncertain.

In addition to clearly *Vedic* works, numerous oral and written compositions, especially in southern India, rival the *Vedas* as sources of Hindu piety. Although many of these are presented as commentaries on the *Vedas*, others have no connection with the *Vedic* corpus, yet they are venerated by local communities as equal to the *Vedas* themselves.

The Upanishads

The *Upanishads* are a major collection of sacred texts that interpret and explain the *Vedas*. Each of them relates to a specific *Veda*. The *Taittiriya Upanishad* expounds the meaning of verses in the *Yajur Veda,* while an interpretation of the *Sama Veda* is found in the *Chandogya Upanishad*. Expositions of the *Rig Veda* are found in various *Upanishads,* such as the *Aitreya Upanishad*. As interpretive texts, the *Upanishads* explain the meaning of not only the Vedas but indirectly all other Hindu literature.

In the *Upanishads*, activist and sacrificial themes of the Vedas, epics, and other Hindu literature discussed below give way to philosophical speculation. Within the *Upanishads* there is no rejection of Vedic or epic themes; rather, there is an interpretation and reinterpretation of these themes. Rituals are often explained allegorically, and ritual actions, like sacrifice, are seen in terms of their symbolic meaning.

Structurally, the *Upanishads* take the form of conversations between the teacher, or guru, and the student, or between a husband and his wife. Less commonly they are seen as discussions between equally informed philosophers. A basic assumption of these conversations is that they are expanding *Vedic* teachings and giving the *Vedas* their true interpretation.

The distinguishing feature of the *Upanishads*, in contrast to the stories of the *Vedas* and other epics or ritual texts, is the quest for truth and philosophical knowledge. Behind this quest is a longing for what becomes known as enlightenment or freedom from the bonds of karma and the wheel of samsara. This ultimate knowledge, according to the *Upanishads*, comes only through the experience of the divine, or enlightenment. The *Upanishads* describe this in terms of the relationship between the divine within the human, Atman, and the ultimate divine being, Brahman, that make a cosmic whole.

Frequently, Atman is described as the human soul, while Brahman is described as God. Although this is a common interpretation, the exact nature of Atman is not so clear. *Atman* may be, and often is, the term used for the human soul. On the other hand, *Atman* may also be used to describe a fragment of the divine that is implanted within humans. Historically, philosophers within the Hindu tradition have interpreted the terms *Atman* and *Brahman* very differently, leaving these terms relatively unclear.

Hindu Epic Literature

Technically the epics are known as *smri*, which means what is remembered and taught. Practically the epics are the main medium for transmitting Hindu beliefs. These probably were composed around 500 AD, although some Hindus and scholars date them back to 500 BC. The texts contain stories of epics that are taught to young children, who often know the broad outlines as well as particular verses by heart. They also play an important role in instructing children in right behavior and ethics.

The shortest of the epics is the *Ramayana,* which forms the basis of plays, dances, and numerous artistic expressions from India to Thailand and Indonesia. The story is relatively simple. The young prince Rama is born in the capital of the kingdom of Kosala, where he has three brothers from different mothers in a polygamous marriage. Unfortunately, the handsome and intelligent young prince falls foul of one of these wives, who is his mother's rival. As a result, on the day of his father's coronation, he is sent into exile to fulfill a promise his father recklessly made to this envious wife.

Although exiling his favorite son breaks his father's heart, he has no choice but to act in this way or break a sacred promise. Undaunted by this event, Rama cheerfully leaves home and lives in the forest accompanied by his beautiful wife, Sita, and a faithful brother, Laksmana, who refuses to leave him. The shock of forcing his son into exile causes his father to die of grief.

At this point in the story another brother, Bharata, who is heir apparent, returns from a journey to find his father dead and his brother in exile. Although he begs Rama to return to the kingdom, it is to no avail. Rama remains in the forest, believing he must fulfill his father's last wish.

Then Rama's beautiful wife is kidnapped by the demon king of Sri Lanka. When she refuses to abandon her husband and remains chaste, the king imprisons her. Devastated by grief, Rama begins to search for his wife with the help of his brother and a band of monkeys led by the divine monkey king Hanuman. With the help of the monkeys, Sita's location is discovered, and an expedition is launched to rescue her. After an epic battle, Rama defeats the evil king and rescues his wife. A series of travails follow when Rama doubts the loyalty and chastity of his wife, who eventually is vindicated by her spiritual goodness and virtue.

Hindus see in this epic all the virtues of a good wife, loyalty between father and son, and numerous other social and spiritual goods. On the surface it is also a rattling good adventure story.

For Hindus, however, there is a deeper spiritual significance with many lessons to be learned.

In one interpretation dating from around the thirteenth century, some Indian Christians see hints of the gospel stories. The sufferings of the faithful wife, Sita, are seen to save humans from evil. Another interpretation describes the trials of Rama and Sita as representing the trials of the human soul. Oher interpretations see Rama as the incarnation of the god Vishnu and understand the story in terms of the relationship of Vishnu to humans. However the epic is interpreted, the monkey god Hanuman plays a crucial role and becomes an object of worship.

The other great epic is the *Mahabharata*. This is an enormously long story about the trials of the descendants of Bharata and the Great War between the Kauravas clan and their close relatives, the Pandavas clan. Central to this epic is a story of the god Krishna and the young prince Arjuna, which forms the basis of the best-known text in Indian literature, the *Bhagavad Gita*, commonly known as the *Gita*.

The *Bhagavad Gita* is regarded by many, including Gandhi, as the most important of all Hindu religious books. Written around 300 AD (some scholars argue it was written as early as 300 BC), the *Gita* tells the story of the interaction of Prince Arjuna with his charioteer who, unknown to him, is actually a manifestation of the god Krishna. Arjuna, a member of the Pandavas clan, is stricken by grief at the thought of slaughtering his cousins in the Kauravas clan. Prior to the battle he becomes so downcast that he begins to discuss his troubles, doubts, and questions with his charioteer.

Most of the *Gita* revolves around this momentous conversation. In it Krishna guides Arjuna to an understanding of the nature of human life and the relationship of the soul to its destiny. Krishna describes the soul as untouched by human senses, thoughts, and actions.

Just as humans change clothing, so too does the soul move from body to body in the cycle of transmigration. Inhabiting numerous bodies that live and die, the soul moves on through time until eventually it is liberated from the vicious cycle of birth and death to which it is bound by the wheel of samsara. The soul never dies, although numerous bodies die. Here the teaching is that the soul is never born, is never killed, and experiences nothing of the trauma of this world, which, in reality, is illusory.

Arjuna must learn not to feel pity, sorrow, or grief. His role is to do his duty. This duty, or dharma, is to fight for righteousness and repudiate cowardice. If he fails in his duty, evil will triumph and his people will be lost. Gradually, as the conversation progresses, Krishna reveals his deity to Arjuna. The young prince is granted a vision of the divine that forms the crowning act of the *Gita*.

Through the *Gita*, Hindu monotheism develops from abstract principles and the theoretical identification of individual gods with the one God into an intensely personal form of devotion. The one cosmic being is identified as a highly personal God who takes an intimate interest in each individual soul. Yet, unlike Christianity, this interest in the individual is an interest in an eternal soul, not a particular person. Consequently, Arjuna learns to detach himself from personal feelings and the cares of this life and to act on an intellectual conviction of what he believes is right for his people, regardless of its effects on himself as a person or on the people he is forced to kill.

Although most Hindus claim that the Vedas are the source of their religious beliefs and practices, the great epics of the *Ramayana* and *Mahabharata* form the practical basis of most Hindu religious life. From the reading of these epics, the presentation of their stories in films and plays, and more recently their appearance on television, Hindus gain entry to the rich mythology and religious teachings of their tradition.

The Dharma Sutras

Two major works provided Hindu rulers and their followers with instruction in government and legal issues. These are the famed

Laws of Manu, composed between the end of the second century BC and end of the second century AD, and the *Artha-Shastra* of Kautilya. These texts outline the duties and techniques of government and are based on a rigid caste system where people are born into a particular strata of society from which they can never escape.

The Puranas

The *Puranas* represent the popular expression of Hindu piety. There are eighteen major Puranas and eighteen minor ones, all of which claim to expound the *Vedas.* They glorify gods, provide lineages, and develop a mythology that supplements the epics. Generally speaking, the *Puranas* are devoted to the virtues of particular gods. For example, the *Vishnu Purana* is written in praise of the god Vishnu and is a product of a particular Vaishnavite religious movement. In this important work, an attempt is made to develop doctrine in such a way that it embraces the entirety of earlier Brahmanic teachings and practices. In this Purana, the five traditional topics of older writings are preserved in six books. The first four and the final book of the *Vishnu Purana* develop traditional materials from classic texts, which are given a consistent Vaishnavite interpretation woven together with a rich devotional mythology.

Only the fifth book contains what may be considered entirely new devotional materials. This Purana begins an account of the creation of the cosmos by the god Vishnu, who is identified with Brahman, who encompasses the whole universe. Vishnu's existence takes many forms. On the one hand, he is pure spirit, *Purusa*; on the other, primary matter, or *Prakriti.* Most important of all he is eternal time, or *Kali,* whose actions separate spirit and matter. Creation therefore becomes the sport of Vishnu, a sacred enjoyment known as *lila,* tied into a series of eternal cycles. These recurring cycles of creation and destruction are called the *Great Yugas* or *Maha Yugas.* Each of them lasts for 4,320,000 human years, which is reduced to 12,000 years in the lifetime of the gods, where one day is equivalent to a human year. All the *Puranas* teach a similar doctrine of creation and destruction based on a cyclic view of time. The entire vision is underwritten by a monistic worldview that sees reality as fundamentally one and all beings as part of this whole. It is based on the *Upanishads*. This religious vision is also theistic and manages to incorporate a personalized god.

The Yoga Sutras

The Yoga Sutras of Patanjali, who lived somewhere between the fourth century BC and the sixth century AD, provide a systematic interpretation of the practice of yoga, making clear the significance of yoga that developed out of the *Upanishads*. In this influential work, yoga is defined as the "mastery or suppression of the mind." The goal of yoga is said to be the attainment of a pure state of consciousness that exists without any of the distractions of normal mental processes or daily life. By the suppression of all mental activity, this refined state is eventually reached.

The Hindu Gods

Avatars, or savior figures, are usually seen in the Hindu tradition as manifestations of the gods Vishnu or Krishna, who enter the world, according to Hindu mythology, to restore order and true knowledge after periods of degradation and decline. This idea of the appearance of God or gods on earth is superficially similar to that of the Christian idea of the incarnation. The big difference between Hindu and Christian teachings is that while Christ is both God and man, the avatars of the Hindu tradition are entirely divine.

Similarities like this have led some Indian Christians to claim that the Hindu tradition is best understood as a reaction to the work of early Christian missionaries. In this view, pre-Christian India had a variety of loosely related local religious cults that, when confronted with the preaching of the gospel, developed their own apologetic that found expression in the great texts of the Hindu tradition. Although this view is rejected by most Western scholars, it probably deserves more study, because it does help to explain some strange similarities between Christianity and the Hindu tradition.

At the top of the Hindu hierarchy of gods is a trinity of beings. These are Brahma, Vishnu, and Shiva, all of which are accompanied by their female consorts. Together these pairs of leading gods represent the vital forces of creation known in Indian thought as *śakti*, or divine power. It is important to note that traditional Indian ways of thinking about the relationship between men and women are different from those in the West. Until at least the sexual revolution of the 1960s, the dominant idea of the female in Western thinking was that of a relatively passive being. In India, however, it is the male who is seen as essentially passive while the female is active. In at least one Indian religious movement, Śaktism, the gods who are the focus of popular piety are depicted as female. In this movement, the figures of Durga, a female warrior figure who often rides on a tiger to slay demons, and Kali, the goddess of time and destruction who is the consort of Śiva, predominate.

An interesting fact about these traditions is that the gods are capable of taking many different forms and, in the case of Durga and Kali, can sometimes be identified with each other. For example, in the *Bhagavad Gita*, Krishna appears as the charioteer of Prince Arjuna. Yet in other stories, Krishna appears herding cows or as a musician. The ability of the gods to take many forms and identities that are sometimes interchangeable has led many Hindu thinkers to argue that all of these forms and all the different gods are simply expressions of one divine essence. They argue that Hinduism is a form of monotheism that uses numerous different stories to express the inexpressible truth about God.

Because the gods play such an important role in Hindu piety, it is important to know something about them and their histories. Using the conventional chronology found in most books about Hinduism, the earliest gods are said to be those referred to in the *Vedas*, particularly the *Rig Veda*. Here we find the worship of nature as befits the interests of a pastoral people. The sun god Surya and the fire god Agni are important here. So too is the wine god Vayu and Indra, the king of the gods who is also the god of thunder and lightning. There is also Varuna, the keeper of the cosmic order.

At the time of the writing of the *Ramayana* and *Mahabharata*, somewhere between 300 BC and 300 AD, the stories of gods were interwoven with those of human heroes. In these later works, various minor Vedic deities like Vishnu and Krishna take on an increasingly important role. Sometime during the fourth to sixth centuries AD, the mother goddess Bharat Mata, or Mother India, was added, and the use of images in worship became common.

In the *Rig Veda*, Indra is perhaps the most important of the gods. He is a warrior god with cosmic powers who frequently wars with other gods. Another important god is Agni, god of fire, who, like Mercury in Greek mythology, is a messenger between humans and other gods. As such the stories of Agni serve to explain the function of sacrifice. Because Agni is the god of fire and a messenger, offerings that human beings burn become messages to the gods. Similarly, the god Soma is both the moon god and a sacred drink that many scholars identify with mushrooms and hallucinogenic substances. Soma is also identified with ecstatic experiences and spiritual insight.

At times, Vedic descriptions of the gods and goddesses, or at least the way they are named and described, blend together. The goddess Sarasviti is the god of rivers, or at least a river god, but has also been described as the god of wisdom and learning. The *Rig Veda* describes Sarasviti as the source of inspired thoughts, truthfulness, beauty, wise words, and dynamism. Later, in the *Brahmanas,* the god Sarasviti becomes identified with speech and the goddess Vac, who is the consort of a creator god Prajapati. As the author of speech, Vac and Sarasviti, with whom Vac is identified, becomes the Word rather like the Logos in Christianity. She's described as "the mother of the Vedas."

To complicate things further, Sarasviti is also identified with Savirti the sun god and Gayatri the singer, who in turn is identified with the ritual formula used during the initiation ceremony of young boys. Gayatri becomes a mantra, or ritual incantation, that is chanted when young boys are given a sacred thread to wear throughout their life, thus marking their transition from childhood to the beginning of manhood and the commencement of their studies.

Throughout the Vedas, the dominant theme is that of sacrificial ritual, or *yajña*, performed in close association with fire. Although major sacrifices are conducted by ritual specialists who chant the hymns and perform sacred actions, other sacrifices belong to the home. In addition to fire sacrifices, offerings that involve eating and drinking, particularly the drinking of the juice of the plant soma, which, as has been observed, many believe to be the juice of hallucinogenic mushrooms, are important.

Philosophically these sacrifices are justified in terms of the preservation of the cosmic order, or *rta*, which implies truth, justice, and the balance of creation. In *Purusa Sūkta*, understood as a hymn to the Supreme Being, the whole of creation is depicted as originating from the primordial sacrifice of the cosmic man.

The Caste System

Probably the most important and contentious feature of the Vedas for social life is the division of society into four classes, or castes. These castes are believed to be rooted in the essential ontology of the universe. This understanding of the ontological structure of society is reinforced by the *Institutes of Vishnu*, where we read in book two that *Brahmins*, Kshatriyas, Vaishyas, and Shudras are the four castes.

The reader is told that the first three castes are the "twice-born." The text then outlines the duties of each caste.

The Brahmins are priests and teachers who form the intellectual elite. These are followed by the Kshatriyas, the warriors and rulers who are the social elite. These two elite groups are followed by the Vaishyas, who constitute the Indian middle class made up of farmers, merchants, and traders. Then there are the Shudras, the huge laboring class. Finally, there is a very large group of people known as Dalits, who are social outcasts. Traditionally they performed menial jobs as street sweepers and toilet cleaners and were shunned by the four castes. Today, as a result of missionary education, many Dalits are well educated and work in areas like computer technology.[1]

These social divisions, or castes, are known as *varanas*, which can also mean "colors." The suggestion is that the classes, or castes, of Hindu society were originally based on racial differences expressed in terms of color. This understanding is reinforced by the fact that the light-skinned people inevitably belong to higher castes than people with darker skin. At its crudest, some critics say that this suggests Hindu social life is based on a form of religiously enforced apartheid.

Most Hindus vigorously reject this suggestion, pointing out that apartheid was a modern notion based on scientific racism, and that among the Tamils some high-caste people are very dark. Nevertheless, it is important to remember that Hindu reformers like Mahatma Gandhi fought hard to abolish the social effects of caste in India. It is also important to note that even today, caste plays a key role in India even though in the West many academics and others play down its importance.

The Hindu Calendar

Hindu piety is closely tied to the Hindu calendar, which, like many religious calendars, is a lunar one. It is divided into twelve lunar months, which vary in length between twenty-nine and thirty-two days. Each month is divided into dark and bright divisions. An extra month is added, rather like the leap year, every three years. In this sense, it is roughly similar to the Western Gregorian calendar.

Hindu Rituals and Piety

The Hindu tradition is both highly philosophical and deeply devotional. Contrary to common expectations, many Hindu philosophers, such as Sankara and Ramanuja, were also deeply devotional. Hindu piety begins in the home, and each home has a place set aside as a shrine to the gods of the household. Sometimes an entire room is devoted to this purpose. More commonly, the images of deities occupy an alcove in one particular room, which is often the kitchen. Offering food, drink, and devotion to the gods the images represent is known as *puja*. Before offering the worship, worshipers are supposed to ritually cleanse themselves.

Ritual cleansing plays an important role in Hindu tradition, where washing and bathing are very important. Before prayer can be offered or sacred words chanted, good Hindus will wash their mouth. Another important aspect of the Hindu tradition is the removal of shoes when entering a temple or even when entering a devout household.

Various forms of ritual purity also affect prayers and other religious rites. Menstruating women, or women who have recently given birth, are ritually impure. So too are people who have touched dead bodies or come in contact with a large variety of unclean things such as blood, urine, or excrement.[2]

Rites of Passage: Birth, Marriage, and Death

The major rites of passage in the Hindu tradition are, as with most other traditions, birth, marriage, and death. Traditionally before birth, prayers are said for the baby, and the gods are asked to give the woman a male child. After birth, mother and child are regarded as ritually impure for ten days. During the birth the Hindu tradition maintains rituals similar to those in medieval Europe. During this time, only midwives and physicians are supposed to have contact with them. Elaborate ceremonies exist, including welcoming the child into the home and whispering the child's name into its right ear. The name given to a child, according to tradition, was always related to the name of a god. But today, Western names are often given to people living in Western countries.

Marriages within the Indian tradition are elaborate communal affairs. Traditionally, all marriages were arranged. Today, many marriages still are arranged even by Christian families. Although modern arranged marriages usually allow the couple to meet beforehand to decide whether they will marry or not, the belief persists within the Hindu tradition that love develops during marriage and is not the basis for marriage. In this sense, marriage is an arrangement between families.

When a person is dying, if they are a good Hindu, they ought to be given a sip of water from the Ganges River. Then they are expected, if at all possible, to chant the name of God. Most modern Hindus believe that after death, the soul moves on to another body and another lifetime. Historically, however, a variety of other options, including a belief in annihilation, existed within the Hindu tradition. After death, the names of God ought to be chanted by the mourners, and passages from the *Bhagavad Gita* are read aloud. In India cremation is common, although for those who can arrange it, water burial in the Ganges is considered a holy act.

According to Hindu custom, people must remain with the body, chanting and praying and reading from the *Gita* to aid the soul and its journey, until cremation takes place. Ideally, cremation ought to occur within twenty-four hours of death. After the funeral, the participants are ritually unclean and need to take ritual baths to purify themselves. Mourning continues between ten and thirty days, during which time the mourners are still considered ritually unclean.

Dietary Laws

Hindu dietary laws are remarkably flexible and vary among families depending on caste, geographic location, and family history. Many Hindus are vegetarian. Others who are not total vegetarians limit the sort of meats they eat to poultry and fish. Within the Hindu tradition, there are various traditional classifications of food. Some foods and drinks, such as alcoholic drinks, are believed to provoke anger. Other foods, such as garlic, are believed to create sexual passions. Most vegetables are believed to produce good living and a healthy lifestyle. In traditional families, men eat their meals before the children and women, but for practical purposes, most Hindus in the West, as well as in modern India, eat and drink together.

Hindu Celebrations

Because the Hindu tradition is essentially a tradition of the home, there are as many celebrations as there are families. As a result, Hindu celebrations vary from area to area, caste to caste, and family to family. Nevertheless, particularly in Western countries, certain major festivals have become common events within Hindu diaspora communities. Probably the most popular feast is the Diwali, or the Festival of Lights, which is celebrated around the fall with lanterns and fireworks. The winter festival of Shivaratri, in praise of the Lord Shiva, which involves dancing, singing, and feasting, is also very popular. So too is the spring festival of Ramanavami, which celebrates the birth of the god Rama. During this festival, plays from the *Mahabharata* are performed, and stories about Rama are read. The Krishna Janmashtami festival is celebrated in the late summer with feasting. A harvest festival, the Sankranthi, is also often observed.

During both Diwali and Sankranthi, gifts are exchanged, making them rather like Christmas.

Because of the eclectic nature of the Hindu tradition, most Hindus have no difficulty celebrating Christmas. Indeed, while some agnostics may object to things like Christmas greetings, Hindus generally respect such celebrations and enjoy them.

Communal Worship

In India, Hindu temples are used on special occasions, such as family and communal celebrations. Increasingly, however, both within Hindu reform movements in India and in the Western world, temples resemble churches. As a result, they become centers where people from India can meet and celebrate common traditions. They also have developed practices similar to Sunday schools to teach their traditions to children. Worship services are held by priests who today often give talks rather like sermons in which they remind worshipers what it means to be a Hindu. During such services, offerings of food and drink are made to images of the deities that are believed to be indwelt by God or the gods.

Conclusion

So far we have provided an overview of the Hindu tradition. In the following chapter we will turn to issues that are problematic and deserve further discussion.

chapter nine

The Enigma of Hinduism

Introduction

As noted at the beginning of the last chapter, the Hindu tradition is probably the most difficult religion to explain because it is complex and rich in art, history, literature, and philosophy, and frankly bewildering to the outsider. What I want to do here is provide you with some issues for thought and discussion that raise questions while offering a way to discuss Christianity with a Hindu or someone from a Hindu background.

The Western Encounter with the Hindu Tradition

Although some knowledge about India and its peoples existed among small groups of people in the West from at least the time of the Greek city-states around 300 BC, it was not until the seventeenth century when Roman Catholic missionaries based in Goa began to interact with educated Hindus that the West more broadly began to encounter Hinduism. Other missionaries and traders increased knowledge of the Hindu tradition during the eighteenth century.

Charles Wilkins (1749–1836) published an English translation of the *Bhagavad Gita* in 1785, making it the first major translation of a Hindu text into English or any European language. A French translation followed in 1787 and a German one in 1802. It was on the basis of this translation that the philosopher Friedrich Wilhelm Joseph Schelling (1775–1854) developed his early philosophy while popularizing Indian thought in Europe.

Wilkins was encouraged in his work by other British Orientalists, such as Sir William Jones (1746–1794) who, like Wilkins, was employed by the British East India Company. Together they created the Asiatic Society of Bengal in 1784 and promoted the publication of Indian literature in India. Later both men returned to Britain where they pioneered the study of ancient India and its sacred scriptures.

The first translation of the *Upanishads* appeared in 1802, when Anquetil Duperron (1731–1805) published a Latin translation of selected texts taken from a Persian translation. Other translations followed, the most important being that of Friedrich Max Müller (1823–1900) in 1879. Müller also arranged the translation of the Vedas and various other Indian texts that were published in his series, *The Sacred Books of the East* (1879–1900).

Before the nineteenth century, few Hindus visited the West. Throughout the nineteenth century, however, a growing number visited Europe and North America to study and work. Prominent among these was Raja Ram Mohan Roy (1772–1833), who introduced the term *Hinduism* to the English language. He died and is buried in Bristol, England. Later, at the World Parliament of Religions held in Chicago in 1893, a number of Hindu speakers made a significant impact, including Swami Vivekananda (1863–1902), who stayed on in the West until 1897. During this time he established Vedanta Centers in New York and London and taught hundreds of Westerners, many of whom became converts.

For centuries Hindus had migrated to places like Indonesia and other parts of Asia as well as to the east coast of Africa. During the nineteenth century, large-scale Indian migrations took place in the form of indentured laborers working in East Africa, South Africa, parts of the Caribbean, Fiji, and even Canada. Although they were discouraged from taking their families with them, their families eventually followed to establish thriving Indian communities in all of these lands.

Small-scale Indian migration to Europe, particularly to Britain, began in the 1930s. During the 1950s the number of immigrants began to grow, and large numbers immigrated to Britain as a result of a recruitment drive by the British government to provide low-paid workers for industry in northern England. Many also came from East Africa where various governments, such as that of Idi Amin (1925–2003), were hostile and sought to expel them. This pattern continued until the late 1970s when new laws began to tighten immigration rules.

A similar pattern of immigration to the United States and Canada occurred with Canada taking a far larger proportion of Indian immigrants than the US. Today Indians can be found across Europe and North America, where there are now thriving Indian communities. The arrival of Indian immigrants has seen the building of Hindu temples and the creation of a network of other religious organizations, the most famous of which is the Hare Krishna movement.

Questions on the Received View of Hinduism

The early European understanding of Indian history promoted by British East India Company officials was based on ancient Hindu texts, particularly the *Rig Veda*. This developed into what is known as the "Aryan invasions theory." Essentially, it teaches that before 2500 BC, India was inhabited by a race of dark-skinned people whose religion we know nothing about, although it probably was similar to later Hinduism.

Then beginning around 2500 BC, the Indian subcontinent was invaded by a light-skinned people who probably were related to the ancient Greeks. These tribes conquered India either in one great wave or through a series of smaller invasions. The dark-skinned race that preceded them was pushed south and, to a large extent, incorporated into what became known as the caste system, with lighter-skinned people at its top. Although there was some initial intermarriage, this seems to have quickly come to an end, and the foundations of Indian society were laid down by a rigid social system that prevented marriage between people of different castes.

To support this theory, scholars appealed to the *Rig Veda*, pointing out that it talked about chariots and warriors as well as many gods who appeared to be remarkably similar to the Greek gods. They also pointed to the *Laws of Manu,* which established the caste system as part of an extensive system of law.

Archaeological support for this theory appeared to be forthcoming with the discovery of the ancient Indus Valley civilization by the Indian Archaeological Survey in 1861. The Indus Valley excavations in the 1920s added support to the idea of Aryan invasions so it was universally accepted. However, in the late twentieth century, further excavations showed that there was no evidence for a violent invasion that caused the destruction of the Indus Valley civilization.

Rather, the evidence showed a sudden collapse due to a major change in the ecological condition that, within a relatively short time, turned a well-watered area into a virtual desert. Cities could no longer support their relatively large populations and collapsed. What caused this change in climate conditions is still a matter of discussion, but the best theory so far, which is supported by archaeological evidence, is that the river system supporting agriculture suddenly dried up. The cause of this appears to have been an earthquake hundreds of miles away that changed the course of the major rivers flowing through the area, leaving dry riverbeds that made agriculture impossible.

Other archaeological excavations across the Indian subcontinent from this time period failed to discover any evidence of major invasions and showed that such things as pottery traditions continued undisturbed for hundreds of years during the time when the Aryan invasions were supposed to have taken place. An increasing number of scholars, but not all, now reject the Aryan invasions theory and are beginning to rewrite the history of the Indian subcontinent.

When this lack of archaeological evidence is taken into account, it becomes clear that many other claims about the Hindu tradition are dubious. For example, the earliest evidence we have for anything like the Hindu religion in India comes from around the fourth century AD.

Some Hindu scholars also recognize the problem their tradition has with its origins and argue, as Nirad C. Chaudhuri does in his book *Hinduism: A Religion to Live By*,[1] that Hinduism is actually a relatively young religion. Chaudhuri and others like him recognize that there are elements of Hindu beliefs dating back before the fourth century, but argue that as a religion, what we know as Hinduism emerged much later than many people claim.

That said, Chaudhuri believes Hinduism offers believers a coherent system of religious thought and practice that has to be taken seriously. A Christian can affirm this observation as correct. Hinduism offers its believers satisfying religious experiences and a rich philosophical tradition to enrich their beliefs. Nevertheless, from a Christian perspective, it fails to meet the two criteria of logical consistency and coherence with reality as we know it as proposed by E. J. Carnell, which is discussed on pages 94–95 above.[2]

History and Hinduism

The great weakness of the Hindu tradition as commonly presented is its history and coherence as a belief system. In many respects, Hindus face a lot of the problems faced by Buddhists. Their philosophy is sophisticated and can intrigue many people, but who can really live by it? Essentially, like Buddhism, it denies our experience of daily life by positing an illusory universe.

Where Hindus have an advantage over Buddhists is that most Hindu systems of philosophy do not deny the self. Instead they accept the existence of individuals who, as spiritual beings, or souls, transmigrate from one body to another after death in an endless wheel of existence. Where Buddhists are perhaps more consistent is in the absence of historical claims as an essential part of their belief system.

Hindus, however, usually make claims about the Vedas and other historical texts that make them far older than Judaism or Christianity. It is this issue that Chaudhuri tries to avoid when he admits that although it is possible to find mention of gods with similar names to later Hindu gods as early as 1370 BC, it is very sketchy and does not show anything like the established system of beliefs we recognize as Hinduism. He concludes that the "conventional date" for the *Rig Veda* "is also pure hypothesis, for which there is no evidence whatever."[3]

When arguments like this are presented to Hindus, the majority, whether or not they know of works like that of Chaudhuri, do not see it as an issue. Their commitment to Hinduism is experiential rather than theoretical, and they do not see a lack of history as a problem because they are not making historical claims. Rather, they live within a Hindu community that they find satisfying. The people who are bothered by it are usually Westerners who are converts or academics who, if not converts, have a strong commitment to the acceptance of the ancient nature of Hinduism.

For anyone who is weighing the merits of Christianity and Hinduism, history is an important issue. Both Christianity and Judaism are grounded in history, and when claims are made about the truth of other religions, it is reasonable to expect the same type of rigorous historical analysis to be applied to these other religious traditions. Seen in this light, the historical claims of the Hindu tradition are shaky at best.

The Hindu tradition is rich in philosophy and communal practices. Yet as the Hindu reformers of the nineteenth century, such as Raja Ram Mohan Roy (1772–1833), Debendranath Tagore (1817–1905), and Dayanand Saraswati (1824–1883) recognized, aspects of Hinduism such as the caste system, child marriage, ritual prostitution, and certain forms of sacrifice are problematic and in need of reform. The problem is that many of these practices lie at the core of Hindu life and thus remain issues today. Kenneth Ingham's *Reformers in India* provides background on the history of these issues and the role of Christian missionaries in opposing such practices.[4]

Caste still exists, as does the practice of sacrifice. In the West, Hindu sacrifices usually involve things like foods and milk offered in a temple to an image of a god. In India, animal sacrifice is common and even human sacrifice of children still exists.[5] This is something most academic accounts of Hinduism avoid discussing, but as Edward Conze pointed out in his seminar at Lancaster University which I attended, a survey of Indian newspapers in English shows that such things are not uncommon.

Although these practices are realities that need to be remembered, it is very important not to lose sight of the fact that India is a subcontinent with a population of more than 1.2 billion people. The majority of contemporary Indians are Hindus who are as shocked and appalled by such sacrifices as any Christian. While one may question certain historic beliefs and practices of Hinduism, one must remember that today the vast majority of Hindus have nothing to do with these ancient practices.

The Indian Christian Tradition

When talking and thinking about the Hindu tradition, it is important to remember that, as in Africa, there is a long and rich Indian Christian tradition that many Indians and others know little about. According to Indian legend, the apostle Thomas was the first Christian evangelist to preach in India, where he established a thriving church. Although the historical details of early Indian Christianity are unclear, an increasing amount of archaeological and other evidence supports this claim, which Westerners have tended to overlook and many early scholars who were anti-Christian Deists ignored.

Today around 2.5 percent of the Indian population is Christian. Yet an ancient church existed in the state of Kerala where St. Thomas is believed to have landed in 52 AD. Whether he did or not is still argued about, but what is certain is that both Eusebius of Caesarea (260–340 AD) and St. Jerome (347–420), who are early church fathers, said that Nathaniel (first century AD), who is named in the Gospel of John and known as St. Bartholomew, pioneered Christian missionary work in India. Eusebius said that Pantaenus of Alexandria (d. 200 AD) also visited Indian churches.

This early manuscript evidence is backed by extensive archaeological finds in India that show a well-established Christian tradition from at least the third century AD. Indian Christianity appears to have flourished and spread across the Indian subcontinent until the seventh century, when it went into decline. Indian Christianity was revived with the arrival of Jesuit missionaries in the seventeenth century. Protestant missionaries followed in the late eighteenth and early nineteenth centuries.[6]

It is reasonable to believe that the Christian tradition in India is at least as old as most forms of European Christianity and much older than Christianity in some parts of northern Europe. Indian Christians have a right to claim that Christianity is a genuinely ancient Indian religion and not a relatively recent European or colonial import. It is important to remind anyone who tends to dismiss Indian Christianity as the result of British intervention in the subcontinent that the British East India Company discouraged missionary activity and tended to promote deism and an appreciation of Hinduism and Islam, not Christianity. The colonial import argument distorts the true history of Christianity in India.

The theories of Indian Christians like M. M. Ninan, whose family claims descent from the earliest Indian converts to Christianity, are worth mentioning. Ninan, a professor of physics, has written numerous books in which he presents a challenging account to the rise of Hinduism. The biggest problem with his work is that he fails to fully document his arguments in anything like a standard academic manner, making it academically unreliable. Nevertheless, his theories are provocative and deserve to be studied and either confirmed or refuted.

Essentially, Ninan argues that the lack of solid archaeological evidence in terms of buildings and inscriptions shows that Hinduism as we know it did not exist before the second century AD. Although he allows for the existence of earlier forms of traditional religion, which he identifies as Aryan Vedic nature worship, as well as Buddhism, Jainism, and Zoroastrianism, all of which can be clearly identified in terms of archaeological and other evidence as existing in India before the time of Christ, he points out that the rise of Hinduism is an enigma.

To explain this, he argues that Christian missionaries were more successful in the early centuries after the death of Christ than has been previously recognized. He points to numerous archaeological discoveries all over the Indian subcontinent which he claims show that early Christian missionaries left recognizable traces of their activities. But because of the dominance of the modern Hindu version of history, these finds have not been taken seriously.

The downfall of early Christianity in India, in his view, was the arrival of Gnostic missionaries from Syria in the third century AD. These missionaries successfully converted existing Christian communities to Gnostic communities. Ninan provides an account of the development of Hinduism by suggesting that the Hindu tradition emerged out of Gnosticism.

This argument is an interesting one and could work as an explanatory model. What is needed is more investigation and careful documentation. Such investigation may show that while Ninan is not entirely correct, his argument that Gnosticism had a profound effect in shaping the consolidation of the Hindu tradition does explain the lack of earlier evidence for a clearly developed Hindu tradition.

Ninan's theory also provides Christians with a way of understanding similarities between Christian and Hindu beliefs that might otherwise be overlooked and shows that the basic impulse of Hindu devotions is a response to real spiritual needs that Christians also recognize. As Christians, we want to show that Christ meets these longings best because his work is grounded in both human experience and history.

Conclusion

The Hindu tradition is arguably the most confusing of all religious traditions. As noted earlier, one can be a Hindu and an atheist, a believer in many gods or a worshiper of one god. The possibilities are endless. When talking with Hindu friends or acquaintances, it is important to find out what they believe before attempting to present the gospel to them. Friendship is by far the best approach, and it will be rewarded.

When you get to know a person, questions may arise about what you believe. Approach things slowly and gently. Find out what your friend or friends believe and ask them to explain their religion to you. Ask a lot of questions and really get to know them and their faith. Only then can you present your understanding of the gospel and in doing so draw attention to the historical evidence for Jesus and his work.

You can compare Christian beliefs to the beliefs of your friends and let them decide which are most likely to be true. This is not easy, but it is well worth the effort and will enrich your faith while giving your Indian friends an understanding of Christianity that might lead them to embrace the Christian way.

chapter ten

The Abramic Tradition

Introduction

Abramic religions trace their ancestry back to the person of Abraham, whose story is found in the book of Genesis in what Christians call the *Old Testament*. The three main Abramic religions are Judaism, Christianity, and Islam. All of them share a common understanding of God as Creator. They also share various related concepts such as creation, the fall, redemption, and the idea of revelation, which, as will be seen, they understand differently. The name Abram is derived from the story of Abraham found in Genesis 11:26–17:5.

Both Judaism and Christianity accept the Hebrew Bible as God's revelation. Christianity adds the *New Testament* while still acknowledging the Hebrew Bible as equally important. But Islam, at least since the tenth century AD, has claimed that both the Hebrew Bible and New Testament are corrupt, and only the *Qur'an* contains authoritative revelation from God. With this in mind, we now turn to a short discussion of the key beliefs of the Abramic tradition.

Because this book is written for Christians, we have not included a separate chapter on Christianity. Anyone wanting more information on Christianity can consult the larger companion textbook, *Understanding World Religions*.[1] In this chapter we will simply review some central teachings of Christianity in relation to other Abramic religions.

Abramic Ideas of Revelation

Most Christians and Jews share a common view of revelation. For them God spoke to humankind through his prophets. They were ordinary men who became extraordinary because God inspired them to proclaim his message to the world. One way of describing this is to say that they both believe God's revelation to humankind takes the form of inspired texts.

The doctrine of inspiration teaches that the *Bible* is the Word of God because it is inspired. Traditional Christians and Jews believe that every word of the Bible in its original autograph was exactly what God intended the prophets to proclaim. More liberal members of both traditions believe that the Bible simply "contains" the word of God. What exactly this means is a matter of dispute but, generally speaking, they agree that the overall message of the Bible is one sent by God. Regardless of how they understand the doctrine of inspiration, both Christians and Jews agree that the people to whom it originally came spoke God's words in their own language in such a way that it reflected their personalities as well as historical and social conditions.

Commenting on the doctrine of biblical inspiration, Princeton theologian B. B. Warfield (1851–1921) wrote:

> The biblical books are called inspired as the divinely determined products of inspired men; the biblical writers are called inspired as breathed into by the Holy Spirit, so that the product of their activity transcends human powers and becomes divinely authoritative. Inspiration is, therefore, usually defined as a supernatural influence exerted on the sacred writers by the Spirit of God.[2]

This belief is based on Bible verses like 2 Timothy 3:16 that reads, "All Scripture is God-breathed," and 2 Peter 1:21, "Prophecy never had its origin in the human will, but prophets, though human, spoke from God as they were carried along by the Holy Spirit."

Muslims have a different understanding of revelation and inspiration. At least since the tenth century AD, they have argued that the doctrine of inspiration embraced by Christians and Jews is misguided because there is no guarantee that even the best-preserved manuscript of the Bible actually contains the Word of God and has not been corrupted by copyists. Instead they distinguish between revelation given to humankind by God through the prophet Muhammad and preserved in the Qur'an and inspiration of the type Christians and Jews talk about, which can be seen in their view in both the life and teachings of the prophet Muhammad and, to a lesser extent, in Christian and Jewish Scriptures.

As a result, Islamic theology makes a sharp distinction between the inspiration of a prophet who speaks for God and the revelation of the Qur'an as recited by Muhammad. In his words and deeds, Muhammad was inspired by God. But when he recited the Qur'an, he recited the literal words of God, which are a unique divine revelation that exists in heaven. Muslims make a distinction between inspired writings like the Bible, and the Qur'an, which they claim is pure revelation without any human intervention. They see the Bible as inferior to the Qur'an.

In trying to understand this, the example of televised election debates is helpful. When viewers saw and heard debates between Mrs. Clinton and Mr. Trump broadcast live on television, or heard them live on radio, they heard the speakers' exact words. When they read about these debates the next day in newspapers, they were given summaries of the key arguments. For Muslims, the Qur'an is the only revelation that can be trusted because it is the actual Word of God.

The Doctrine of Creation and Its Implications

The doctrine of creation sets Abramic religions apart from Yogic religions. Following the Hebrew Bible, Abramic religions teach that God brought the entire universe into existence by an act of will.

He did not re-form preexisting matter or change a part of himself to make material things. Rather, "what is seen was not made out of what was visible" (Heb. 11:3). As the Nicene Creed states, God is "the Creator of heaven and earth, and of all things visible and invisible."

The Abramic tradition conceives of creation as far more than just an original creative act that started the universe. The Scriptures recognized by Christians, Jews, and Muslims agree that the original act of creation involves God's *continuing* providence as well. God made the universe and continues to uphold it by his will. The universe is governed by God's laws, which regulate every aspect of creation. God is not dependent on his creation. It is dependent on God. He is sovereign, and everything is subordinate to him. He is absolute, and everything else is relative. All people owe their existence to God. We are finite, he is infinite. An absolute distinction exists between the creature and the Creator.

When God created the universe, he pronounced it good. God's original creation was without blemish. Our present state and the presence of evil and suffering in the world were not part of God's original intention. They resulted from human disobedience to God, which had cosmic implications. Christians call this act of disobedience "the fall."

The Present State of the World

Abramic religions differ in the way they understand the situation of humans in the world. In response to the question, "How could a good God have created a world with so much suffering and evil it?" Christians respond by explaining that while the original creation was good, its perfection was disrupted by an original act of human rebellion against God. This they call "the fall." Christian theology argues that all humans are born into a state of rebellion and are sinful by nature and inclined to sin.

The doctrine of the fall as an event that caused all humans to be born into a state of rebellion against God is rejected by both Jews and Muslims. They see humans as born without inherited sin who only become sinners when they knowingly disobey God. For them the story of Adam and Eve explains the human condition, but without the ongoing consequences Christians believe are implied by the story.

Obedience of both Jews and Muslims to God in the present life is what is important in terms of everyday living and our eternal future. Today various groups of Jews see this in different ways. The vast majority of Muslims share the common belief that humans are commanded to obey God's will as revealed in the Qur'an, and only total submission to the teachings of Islam satisfies God's demands.

Christians trace the fall to chapters 2 and 3 of the book of Genesis, which relate the story of the garden of Eden. Adam was told that he could eat of any tree except the tree of the knowledge of good and evil because "when you eat from it you will certainly die" (Gen. 2:16–17). Disregarding this command, Adam and Eve ate the fruit, discovered their mistake, and lost communication with God. Sin and death entered the world.

What does this biblical account teach us about the human condition? The Christian answer is that Adam and Eve were given freedom within the limits of human finitude and were placed in an ideal environment. They were warned about the danger of death and were otherwise left to explore the world. But they soon disobeyed God, setting into motion the whole panorama of human history as we know it.

The central theme of the story is distrust. Adam and Eve desired the knowledge of good and evil that would make them like God. This suggests not only that they were discontented with their dependent status as finite creatures but also that they desired independence gained through knowledge apart from God rather than through growth, thought, and trust in God.

If this interpretation is correct, the story symbolizes the ever-present human desire for magical shortcuts to knowledge and power at the expense of trust and understanding. At the heart of the

Christian view of the fall is the human desire for sudden and total freedom and power, unrestricted by the limits of the human condition. As we have seen, this is precisely what the Yogic religions claim to offer their followers. The Bible, however, presents the fall as an act of unrestricted self-indulgence based on the impossible desire to be like God. Instead of leading to freedom, it resulted in bondage.

Both Judaism and Islam deny this understanding and claim that all humans are born free and only later do they choose to obey or disobey God. Then when disobedience occurs, it can be rectified by good works and a renewed obedience to the laws of God.

Christians believe that the cosmic dimensions of this original disobedience were so great that the only way humans can be restored to fellowship with God is through an act of redemption that God undertook through the life and work of Jesus Christ.

Redemption and Salvation

Together with the fall, the incarnation and the death and resurrection of Jesus are the central doctrines of the Christian faith. The *New Testament* teaches Christians that God took upon himself the responsibility for human sin and became a man in the person of Jesus. It was Jesus' sacrificial death on the cross and his triumphant resurrection from the dead that overcame human sin and reconciled all those willing to trust in God and his redeeming act to God himself.

The Christian notions of creation, the fall, and redemption fit well with Western attitudes toward science and knowledge. The notions grant knowledge and choice within the confines of God's universe but dictate that since humans are not granted ultimate or godlike knowledge, their pursuit of knowledge can never be complete. These teachings do not allow us to rest in the comfort of having attained union with the One as some believers in Yogic religions do. This disallows the metaphysical stagnation found in some Eastern religions.

The Christian tradition thus emphasizes not *being*, except in the sense of being at peace and bearing the image of God, but rather *becoming*. It entails a pursuit of knowledge and exploration that is never-ending for humanity and in which we will always be able to experience growth and development. Further, it teaches that true obedience to God's law depends on our relationship to God and rests on each individual's conscience. The enforcement of laws by the state and communal standards, however helpful it may be, is only part of the story. This is because someone may live in outward obedience to the Law, but inwardly hate it and nurture rebellion against God in their heart. In other words, Christians obey God out of love in the recognition that he first loved and redeemed them. Their obedience is driven by love, not fear or the hope of heavenly rewards.

By contrast, both Judaism and Islam see human salvation coming about through obedience to God's laws in this life without a savior or anything like the Christian understanding of redemption. For them, believers earn their redemption though obedience, which is a duty that brings heavenly rewards.

Faith in the Abramic Religions

Christians believe that the way humans reenter a living relationship with God is through faith. Faith is the act of trust based on knowledge of God and his deeds revealed in the Bible. It is not a blind leap into the unknown, but a confident step into enlightenment about the nature and love of God. Faith is thus the opposite of doubt and magical power. Faith is to redemption what magic and doubt are to the fall. It frees us of anxiety because it entails accepting our identity as creatures made in God's image. This distinctively Christian understanding of faith is found in the story of Abraham, who left the security of Ur of the Chaldees to become a wanderer and nomad in response to God's call.[3] Christian faith is an expression of trust in God that leads to a new way of life based on a living relationship with God.

In sharp contrast to the Christian view of faith, both Judaism and Islam stress the importance of law. In their view, humans are not fallen creatures; rather, they are free beings who may or may not do good or evil depending on their wills. Since the human will is fickle, only God's law acts as a constraint, and it has to be maintained and applied to human life through communal standards and governmental enforcement of laws based on a correct interpretation of God's revelations.

For Christians, such obedience to prove one's righteousness is legalism that leads to the observance of "a religious festival, a New Moon celebration, or a Sabbath day," which are justified by appeals to what Paul calls "hollow and deceptive philosophy, which depends on human tradition."[4] *New Testament* writers condemn ritual observances as a form of bondage to the law.[5]

The modern beliefs in the importance of the individual and in essential human freedoms are arguably rooted in the Christian tradition, but in secular form, they lack the inner constraints that Christianity demands. According to the *New Testament*, Christians are free, but this freedom is limited by God's law. Christians are free to choose when to act in accordance with God's revealed will. The difference between this view and that of both Jews and Muslims is that it is individual Christians, relying on conscience, their knowledge of biblical teachings, and constant self-reflection, who apply God's law and will to their own lives. Even though conscience plays a role in the lives of Jews and Muslims, their morality is essentially communal in nature and governed by laws that regulate every aspect of life.[6]

The Importance of Community

A concern with community is another hallmark of the Abramic tradition. In Judaism and Islam, community is clearly identified with ethnic, national, or religious observance regulated by priests, as it was in Christianity until the Reformation. Luther and the Reformation emphasized the importance of faith and led many Christians to return to a concept of community found in the New Testament. This stresses the idea of the fellowship of true believers sharing a common faith in an essentially hostile and unbelieving world.

Prophetic Leadership

The question of authentic leadership and religious authority is clearly important in assessing religions. Religions of the Yogic tradition revere gurus, many of whom gain complete authority over their disciples. They offer an experiential way of salvation that is rooted in beliefs found in their various scriptural traditions, but is not limited to the teachings or experiences of those traditions. Gurus are allowed to innovate and introduce new understandings of their faith.

Abramic religions have no gurus. Instead they recognize the prophet as a key figure who transmits God's messages to humans. Prophets differ from gurus in that the prophet claims to declare the word of God, which is then tested against earlier revelations made by other prophets as to whether it comes to pass.

In Christianity and Judaism, most prophets after the time of Moses take existing revelation and apply it to particular situations. In the process they remind God's people of their failures and call on them to restore their relationship with God. Islam believes Muhammad is the last and authoritative prophet who calls all people to submission to God's law as revealed in the Qur'an.

Conclusion

Despite their similarities and claims to share a common source for their religions, the three main Abramic religions hold different views about the nature of scripture and the relationship of humans to God. This is most clearly seen in the use of the term *father* in relation to God.

In Judaism, the term *father* is used of God, but largely as a metaphor. It is not understood literally or metonymically. The term is not used as a name for God but rather as a title that has to be used carefully and with great respect to express the fact that God created all things.

Muslims reject the use of the term *father* in reference to God. Instead they see God as the creator, custodian, helper, and protector of humans, who is both compassionate and merciful yet all-powerful and all-knowing. To talk of God as father is seen as verging on the blasphemous and something that ought not to be done, because it is far too familiar and reduces the dignity of God.

In contrast, Christians speak of God as father as a way of expressing and understanding his relationship to both his Son, Jesus Christ, and the Holy Spirit as well as to the creation, humans, and individual believers. It testifies that God exists in Trinity as Father, Son, and Holy Spirit and is the Creator of all things.

For Christians, the term *father* conveys the reality of God's love to humankind seen in the life and death of Jesus, who, as the creeds proclaim, is God's only begotten Son. It is used as a metaphor, and metonym, that expresses the ultimate reality of God's person, making it the most important of God's names.[7]

Christians believe they are the children of God, by both creation and adoption. Christian teaching about the fatherhood of God is an expression of God's love and of the possibility for individuals to enter into a personal relationship with their Creator that sets Christianity apart from the other Abramic religions.

chapter eleven

The Travails
of Judaism

Introduction

If the Hindu tradition is difficult to discuss because of its complexity, Judaism is hard to talk about today because of World War II and the Holocaust. From the time of the Enlightenment until the late nineteenth century, a steady stream of converts had turned from Judaism to Christianity. Today such conversions are unthinkable to many Jews. To understand this, we need to look at the history of the Jews in some detail.

The Jewish Story

What makes Judaism different from other ancient religions is that, as with Christianity after it, the historical narratives contained in the Jewish Bible, which we will refer to as the Hebrew Bible, are understood to be true accounts of what happened in history. At their core, the stories about Jewish origins have actually happened at specific points of time in particular geographic locations. They are not legends, sagas, or myths of a fictitious nature. These events recorded in the Hebrew Bible give Judaism its dynamic structure, which over the millennia shaped the life and thought of individuals and an entire people.

For Jews, their Bible has three parts, beginning with the Pentateuch, or five books of Moses. The second part is known as "the Prophets," which is divided into two sections. The first section includes the books of Joshua, Judges, Samuel, and Kings, while the second consists of the books of Isaiah, Jeremiah, Ezekiel, and the twelve remaining minor prophets. Finally, the third part is known as "the Writings" and contains the books of Psalms, Proverbs, Job, Song of Solomon, Ruth, Lamentations, Ecclesiastes, Esther, Daniel, Ezra, Nehemiah, and Chronicles. Many biblical books that Christians call "historical," such as the books of Kings, are identified as prophetic works by Jews.

Most Jews recognize the importance of a number of extrabiblical books known as the *Apocrypha*. These include such books as Tobit, Judith, 1–2 Maccabees, Ecclesiasticus, and the Wisdom of Solomon. They are not included in the Jewish Bible itself because the rabbis considered them repetitious or believed that their teachings were not entirely consistent with Judaism. Others were excluded because they were regarded as being too "modern." Because some of these books were included in the Septuagint, a second-century-BC translation of the Jewish Scriptures into Greek, they acquired a degree of authority among Greek-speaking Jews and later Christians.[1]

The Jewish Understanding of History

Against the background of the Torah—which in rabbinic literature means the Law of Moses—the stories of creation, Adam and Eve, Noah, Abraham, and Moses form a pattern of events related to the birth of the Jewish people as a covenant people bound to God. These stories have two main themes: The first is the establishment of an "everlasting covenant" by God with Abraham and his legitimate descendants found in Genesis 17:1–12. The second concerns the giving of the Law to Moses as the outworking of the covenant and the formation of Israel as a distinct people. These are related in Exodus 1–19.

The remainder of the Hebrew Bible tells the story of the development of the Jewish people as a distinct society under God. It relates their trials and tribulations over the centuries and is a story of both devotion and apostasy. Of obeying God and prospering and, alternately, of disobedience leading to judgment. The history recorded in the *Hebrew Bible* is one of ups and downs, periods of piety and rebellion, until at last God promises a Messiah who will save his people and make them into the people he intended them to become.

The story tells how after the children of Abraham took refuge in Egypt, they were enslaved until God sent Moses, who led them into the promised land. There the Israelites lived in the area we know today as Palestine in a loose confederation of tribes that eventually formed a kingdom, which in turn divided into the northern kingdom of Israel and the southern kingdom of Judah. Israel was conquered and destroyed by the Assyrians in 722 BC. Judah submitted to Assyrian rule, continuing as a tributary state until it was conquered between 598 and 586 BC by the Babylonians, who destroyed the city of Jerusalem and its temple, which had become the center of Jewish piety and life. They then enslaved the Jewish people who, for the next seventy years, lived as exiles in Babylon. Seventy years later, following the conquest of Babylon by Persian emperor Cyrus the Great in 538 BC, the remaining Jews were allowed to return to Judah and rebuild Jerusalem and its temple. This was done by two great leaders, Nehemiah and Ezra, who reestablished the covenant of obedience with God.

Judaism underwent further changes following the conquest of the entire Near East by a Macedonian, Alexander the Great (356– 323 BC). His attitude toward the Jews was one of tolerance. After his death, Judea became a province of Egypt ruled by Alexander's general, Ptolemy.[2] Later it was annexed by the kingdom of Syria and its rulers, who were Greek in origin. One of their kings, Antiochus IV Epiphanes, determined to unify his empire religiously and sought to suppress traditional Jewish religious worship by transforming the

Jerusalem temple into a Greek temple. This led to a successful Jewish rebellion led by the priestly Maccabee family and the independence of Judah.[3]

In the period that followed, various new Jewish groups, such as the Pharisees and Sadducees, emerged. The Pharisees stressed obedience to tradition and religious observations. The Sadducees promoted a modernizing form of Judaism based on an admiration for all things Greek. Various other groups of scribes and teachers like those encountered in the New Testament also developed.

Squabbles among political parties led to civil war, which the Roman general Pompey was called on to resolve in 63 BC. Judea became a puppet state of Rome with Roman advisers guiding the policies of a nominally Jewish king. The most important of these Jewish kings was Herod the Great (37–4 BC). These developments led to the emergence of various apocalyptic movements that called for the expulsion of the Romans from Judah and the establishment of the kingdom of God on earth.

After the death of Herod, the Romans assumed direct control of the country. As a result, Jewish rebellions grew in Palestine and spread throughout nearby Roman provinces, including Egypt, where Jews came into conflict with both the Roman authorities and local Greeks.

The Roman emperor Claudius (10 BC–54 AD) attempted to bring to an end the spreading conflicts between Greeks, Jews, and Romans in Egypt and Palestine. He ended direct Roman rule over Judea, allowing it to become a client kingdom under King Agrippa I. When Agrippa died in 44 AD, the area exploded with apocalyptic movements, riots, revolts, massacres, and what today we would call ethnic cleansing caused by tensions between Galileans, Greeks, Samaritans, and Jews. The countryside rapidly became dangerous with robbers and "freedom fighters" terrorizing travelers.

Things came to a head in 67 AD when the Jewish sect known as Zealots seized control of Jerusalem, massacring its Jewish Roman sympathizers. The Romans invaded the area in 68 AD, led by the Roman general Titus as commander of the Jewish campaign. Jerusalem was besieged, and in 70 AD the city fell to the victorious Romans. Titus laid it waste, destroying the Jerusalem temple and severely punishing the Jewish population, many of whom were either enslaved or sent to the arena to face certain death. Finally, in 74 AD, Masada, the last Jewish rebel fortress, fell to the Romans.

According to Jewish legend, the inhabitants of Masada resisted Roman assaults before eventually committing suicide when Roman victory seemed assured. Many historians doubt the suicide story, believing the rebels were captured and enslaved. In the twentieth century, the Masada story became one of the foundation myths of the modern state of Israel. Historians estimate that around one million Jews died during the entire rebellion and its brutal suppression by the Roman legions that ended at Masada. After the Roman victory, biblical Judaism as developed in the *Hebrew Bible* came to an end.

Despite these traumatic defeats, or perhaps because of them, Jewish rebellions continued for several centuries throughout the Roman world. The most significant in shaping long-term attitudes toward Jews in the Roman world, particularly in the Greek-speaking areas, was the Jewish revolt in Cyprus that lasted from 115 to 117 AD.[4] Jewish rebels captured and sacked the city of Salamis, where they slaughtered the Greeks.[5] During the entire revolt, between 200,000 and 500,000 Greeks and Romans were butchered and rumors spread throughout the Roman world about Jewish atrocities. The result was that Jews became associated with terrorism and were seen as people capable of the grossest cruelties against their enemies. In modern terms, the Romans viewed the Jews like Americans view Islamic terrorists.

A second serious revolt occurred in Palestine in 132 AD under the leadership of Simon Bar Kochba. It was provoked by Emperor Hadrian, who embarked on a colonization program that depopulated Judea of Jews and repopulated it with Greeks and Romans.

He outlawed Judaism in the Roman Empire, but after his death in 138 AD, this last decision was reversed. These repeated defeats led the surviving Jews of Judea to reconcile themselves to the Romans, leading to one of most unexpected and significant religious transformations in history. It led to the creation of a new Judaism by Jewish scholars and leaders.

Jewish scholars made scholarship the central feature of Jewish worship and virtually outlawed apocalyptic interpretations of the Jewish scriptures. This redirection of Judaism worked, and they were able to convince their Roman political masters that the encouragement of Jewish scholarship was in their best interests.

During this time, Jewish scholars developed a system of biblical interpretation based on a set of rules known as the *Mishnah* and an interpretative corpus called the *Talmud*. The Mishnah was compiled around 200 AD and is a series of rules divided into six subdivisions: seeds, feasts, woman, damages, holy matters, and purities. From the second century AD, further guides to understanding and applying the teachings of the Hebrew Bible and Jewish traditions were developed by Jewish scholars to explain and apply the Mishnah.

Many of these interpretations were eventually compiled into what became known as the Talmud. The *Jerusalem Talmud*, as it was known, came into being in the fourth century AD. The fifth century saw the production of the *Babylonian Talmud*. The Talmud developed the implications of the Hebrew Bible as presented in the Mishnah. In the Talmud, contradictions are harmonized, legal issues are discussed, and an enormous amount of legendary, theological, and exegetical material, often suitable for preachers, is presented. These texts preserve discussions in an almost shorthand form, giving the essence of arguments and creating endless problems of interpretation that have occupied Jewish scholars until the present.

The discussions of rabbis on these matters are filled with passion and great profundity. The ability to argue and interpret texts became of crucial importance for Jewish life. Yet despite such discussion, conclusions were left open to allow students to reach a decision for themselves. Just like lawyers today, many Jewish men went through rigorous training that required them to remember not only examples discussed as cases in the Talmud but also the arguments about those cases and the best ways of presenting their own views. Rabbis went through similar, but more rigorous, training. Judaism developed an extensive educational system based on local congregations in cooperation with specialized rabbinic academies that created an education-stressed ethos.

Jewish Communities and Sects

Around the seventh century AD, Judaism developed into two major groups, the Sephardic Jews of Spain and the Ashkenazi Jews of northern Europe. Within these communities, philosophy, mysticism, and occasional fundamentalist movements could be found. Judaism defined itself not as a creed, as was the Christian and to a lesser extent Muslim practice, but as a way of life. At the core of traditional, or rabbinic, Judaism was what Michael Fishbane calls "the matrix of traditional Jewish life,"[6] which was kept alive by liturgical practices, communal involvement, and the daily life of Jewish families.

Living in what were often hostile and potentially dangerous environments, Jews in both Christian and Muslim countries looked inward to their own communities for solace and protection. These were traumatic times that created memories of "tears and martyrdom."[7] In Muslim lands, Jews and Christians alike shared the status of *dhimmitedu*, or second-class citizens, protected by the law, but not as well protected as the Muslims to whom they were subservient. In Christian lands, Jews were normally but not always protected by secular rulers and church authorities against the whims of an unstable and ill-educated populace. In both geographic areas, the situation of Jews was at best precarious.

Jewish isolation from the surrounding society brought about

the acceptance of "love and care for fellow Jews" as a central value of Judaism based on the belief that "all Jews are responsible for one another."[8] Perhaps more than anything else, this principle held Jews together over the coming, difficult centuries.

The origin of the term *Sephardic* is unknown, but the term became identified with Jews living in the Iberian Peninsula until they were expelled from Spain by Ferdinand and Isabella in 1492. At that time, the majority of Sephardic Jews took refuge in Muslim lands, moving to Constantinople, North Africa, or Egypt. Others settled in Portugal or emigrated to northern Europe, particularly the Netherlands, where Amsterdam became a Jewish center.[9]

Ashkenazi Jews originated in northern Europe, particularly in German-speaking lands in the tenth century. Later they spread to the Netherlands, Poland, Russia, and eastern Europe. They distinguished themselves educationally and professionally. Initially, some were moneylenders, advisers to local rulers, and tax collectors. Later, as the times allowed, Jewish men took up other professions, becoming doctors and lawyers.[10]

The main differences between Ashkenazi and Sephardic Judaism are in the liturgy and cultural practices within families. As far as cultural practices are concerned, the Sephardic Jews reflect aspects of Arabic culture, while Ashkenazi Jews were strongly influenced by German culture. Today approximately 17 percent of Jews throughout the world are non-Ashkenazi, the majority of these being Sephardic. In Israel, however, the number of Sephardic Jews is around 50 percent, making the Jews of Israel significantly different from many other Jewish communities throughout the world.[11]

Jewish Philosophy and Mysticism

From at least the time of the Hellenized Jewish scholar Philo of Alexandria (20 BC–50 AD), Jews have taken a close interest in philosophy. The most famous of all Jewish philosophers is Moses

Maimonides (1135–1204), who was one of the great medieval exponents of Aristotle and author of *Guide for the Perplexed*.[12] As a good Aristotelian, Maimonides argued that God is purely spirit and that his existence can be known by following Aristotelian logic. He believed in the resurrection of all people after death but was skeptical about the meaning of prophecy. He also sought to preserve Torah and defend it against criticism. Maimonides provided Jews with a creed written in poetic form, which contained the following thirteen points:

1. The belief in the existence of the Creator, be He blessed, who is perfect in every manner of existence and is the Primary Cause of all that exists.
2. The belief in God's absolute and unparalleled unity.
3. The belief in God's non-corporeality, nor that He will be affected by any physical occurrences, such as movement, or rest, or dwelling.
4. The belief in God's eternity.
5. The imperative to worship Him exclusively and no foreign false gods.
6. The belief that God communicates with man through prophecy.
7. The belief that the prophecy of Moses our teacher has priority.
8. The belief in the divine origin of the Torah.
9. The belief in the immutability of the Torah.
10. The belief in divine omniscience and providence.
11. The belief in divine reward and retribution.
12. The belief in the arrival of the Messiah and the messianic era.[13]
13. The belief in the resurrection of the dead.[14]

After his death, Maimonides' Creed came under attack from other Jewish scholars who argued that Judaism ought not embrace a creed that made too many concessions to Christians and Muslims. For them, Judaism was a way of life rather than an abstract expression of belief.[15]

Since then Judaism has produced many philosophers, the most famous being Moses Mendelssohn (1729–1786). His importance within Judaism can be summed up in the saying, "From Moses, to Moses, there is none like Moses." The meaning of this is that Moses of the Bible, Moses Maimonides, and Moses Mendelssohn form a continuous Jewish intellectual and practical tradition. Moses Mendelssohn aimed to equip Jews to compete intellectually with their contemporaries. To do this, he took the best in modern Western scholarship of his time, particularly German scholarship, and used it to defend Judaism. In doing so he created a form of Judaism that reflected the ethos of the Enlightenment.[16] This tradition continues to the present and was represented in the twentieth century by such figures as Martin Buber (1878–1965).[17] Interestingly, all but one of Mendelssohn's grandchildren converted to Christianity. Perhaps the most famous of these is composer Felix Mendelssohn Bartholdy (1808–1847). His oratorio *Paulus*, or *St. Paul*, uses the conversion of the apostle Paul to express his own feelings about becoming a Christian.[18]

Jewish mystical movements existed around the time of Christ, particularly in cities like Alexandria, where Neoplatonism flourished, but it is not until the European Middle Ages that we can form a clear idea about Jewish mystical movements. Attempts to reconstruct earlier mystical movements, often associated with groups like the Essenes, fail because of a lack of documentary evidence.

Jewish mysticism flourished in the Middle Ages when it grew out of earlier rabbinic speculations based on the study of biblical texts. For example, the book of Ezekiel provided a rich depository of symbols and imagery for mystical thinkers. Ezekiel's visions, including that of a chariot, were believed to give insight into the divine nature of God.[19] These visions enabled mystics to enter the spiritual realm through practices that brought on ecstasy, visions, and out-of-body experiences and could be promoted by rigid ascetic practices such as fasting, ritual purity, and magical chants.

The second-century text *Sefer Yetsirah*, or *Book of Creation*, fueled the growth of Jewish mysticism. It taught that God created the universe following thirty-two mystical pathways cosmically bound to the twenty-two letters of the Hebrew alphabet and ten emanations from God himself. Many of these ideas originated philosophically in the teachings of Plato and contributed to what medievalists called the "Great Chain of Being."

The rabbis who promoted these views saw themselves as members of a secret tradition that was embedded within the chain of being and found in the Talmud by those who knew how to look for it. They saw creation and the whole of life as a cosmic struggle for salvation and freedom from evil that would end with the establishment of the messianic kingdom by God himself. Medieval Jewish mysticism flourished in Germany, southern France, and Spain. Such movements became immensely popular until the disastrous millenarian group known as the Shabbatean movement, led by Shabbatai Zevi (1626–1676), developed in Poland during the seventeenth century. It had a demoralizing effect on many Jewish communities after its leader converted to Islam. As a result, the very core of Jewish mysticism appeared threatened. In this situation, the Hasidic movement arose with a message of personal piety and salvation.[20]

The founder of Hasidism was Israel ben Eliezer (1700–1760), who acquired the name Baal Shem Tov. Hasidic traditions say that he was born in Poland and as a young man traveled to the Carpathian Mountains where he acquired spiritual wisdom. In the 1730s he began a tour of various Jewish communities where he was said to have performed miracles and recruited disciples.

Following his death, the Hasidic movement spread throughout Poland, the Ukraine, and Lithuania. Over the years it encountered growing opposition from the rabbinate. Eventually, however, the persistence of the movement led to its recognition by both Jewish and secular authorities. Hasidism made two major innovations within the Jewish tradition. First, it allowed ordinary people to achieve religious ecstasy through joyful worship, singing, and dancing as liturgical acts in anticipation of the messianic kingdom. Second, it introduced a new form of leadership into the Jewish tradition. This was the *rebbe*, who was a charismatic figure very different from the traditional rabbi. Within Hasidism, the *rebbe* was a superior spiritual being who gained his authority from spiritual experiences. The movement also developed the practice of pilgrimage to the site of the graves of famous *rebbes* and in doing so gave the movement a dynamic sense of community. Nevertheless, the Hasidic movement was looked down upon by many educated Jews and seen as an embarrassment by the sophisticated Ashkenazi Jews of German-speaking lands. Not until the twentieth century, largely as a result of the writings of Martin Buber, did Hasidism come into its own as a religious movement compatible with the modern world.[21]

Finally, it is important to note that in many parts of Europe and other places, either by choice or because of local laws, Jews lived in restricted areas and ghettos, cut off from their non-Jewish neighbors. They were often victims of discriminatory laws and varying degrees of persecution.

Jewish Piety

Beyond doubt, the Sabbath is by far the most important of all Jewish holy days and ritual observances. Remembering the Sabbath is what makes Israel, Israel. The Sabbath begins at sundown every Friday evening and ends with sundown on the following day. In recognition of the commencement of the Sabbath, the senior Jewish woman in the home lights ritual candles. The senior man then recites the ritual prayer over the bread and wine at the beginning of the evening meal, which joyfully celebrates the coming of the Sabbath.

Many Jews, particularly the Orthodox, attend synagogue before such activities take place. Others, particularly members of Conservative and Reform congregations, attend a late-evening service. For all three groups, and various other minor, or sectarian, Jewish groups, Sabbath worship also takes place the following day, that is, on Saturday. Orthodox Jews refrain from all forms of work on the Sabbath and, if they are very strict, do not even turn on a light or drive a car. Other groups are more lenient in their interpretation of Sabbath laws, or, as in the case of some smaller sectarian groups, even stricter than the Orthodox. The Sabbath concludes with a short ceremony just before sundown on Saturday when a lit candle is extinguished in a glass of wine and a box of spices is passed around to family members for them to taste and smell. The symbolism of this is that the sweetness of the Sabbath is passing away.

The Jewish calendar is based on the belief that the creation took place 3,760 years before the birth of Christ or, as most Jews would say, before the Common Era. To know which Jewish year it is, all you have to do is take a given year and add 3,760 to it. For example, the year 2000 in the Jewish calendar was the year 5760, while the year 2020 is the Jewish year 5780. The Jewish calendar combines the lunar and solar calendars with months that vary in length between twenty-nine and thirty days. To harmonize the calendar with the rotation of the Earth around the sun, it works on a nineteen-year rotation with twelve years of twelve months and seven years of thirteen months. These monthly leap years are the eleventh, fourteenth, seventeenth, and nineteenth years. Consequently, there is no relationship between the Jewish months and the secular Western ones. The Jewish months and their secular equivalents are as follows:

Tishrei: September–October
Cheshvan: October–November
Kislev: November–December
Tevet: December–January

Shevat:	January–February
Adar:	February–March
Nisan:	March–April
Tyar:	April–May
Sivan:	May–June
Tammuz:	June–July
Av:	July–August
Elul:	August–September

Although Jewish holidays are regular within the Jewish calendar, they vary considerably in terms of the secular Western calendar. Because the Jewish day begins at sunset, it is reckoned differently than the secular Western way of counting a day.[22]

The Jewish calendar begins with Rosh Hashanah, which commemorates the creation of the world and the opening of the book of life by God. It begins on the first day of the month Tishrei. Unlike most other Jewish holidays, which are essentially family based, this is a communal holiday celebrated in the synagogue. It also marks the beginning of the Jewish New Year and a ten-day cycle, known as the days of awe, when practicing Jews engage in self-examination and reflection.

This is followed by Yom Kippur, or the Day of Atonement, which occurs at the end of the ten-day cycle of reflection connected with Rosh Hashanah. On this day Jews come to terms with themselves and make peace with any they have wronged. They are expected to fast and pray, asking God for forgiveness. This is the holiest and most solemn day in the Jewish year.

More recently the old celebration of Hanukkah has been revised to become a sort of Jewish Christmas in North America. It is a time of joy and blessing and is symbolized by the eight-branch menorah, or candlestick, which holds nine candles, four on each side and one in the center. Hanukkah is a celebration of light in remembrance of a miracle believed to have occurred at the time of the Jewish revolt against Syrian domination. According to legend, the Maccabees relit the sacred lamp in the temple that had been extinguished in an attempt to suppress Judaism. When they relit it, they only had enough oil for one day, yet miraculously the lamp burned for eight days, giving them time to purify the new oil required to resupply the lamp. The celebration is a time of relaxation and of fun and games during which Christmas-type gifts are exchanged.

Far more solemn is Pesach, the feast of the Passover, which occurs in the month of Nisan to commemorate the liberation of the children of Israel from Egyptian bondage. During the eight days of this feast, Jews eat unleavened bread called *matzot*. They also take part in a special meal, the Seder, where they retell the story of their ancestors' escape from Egypt. During this meal, symbolic foods are eaten to remind Jews of the various aspects of the exodus story.

Another joyful, or at least lighthearted, feast is Purim on the fourteenth day of the month of Adar. Purim celebrates the story of the Jewish heroine Esther, who married the king of Persia in the fifth century BC. Neither the king nor his courtiers knew that Esther was Jewish. When one of the king's advisers, Haman, plotted to murder the Jews, Esther was able to save her people, and it was Haman who was executed. For many modern Jews, this feast is like Halloween with a religious message.

On the sixth day of the month of Sivan, Jews observe Shavuot, a harvest festival that celebrates the reception of the Ten Commandments by Moses. This feast centers on a family meal and the reading of the *Torah*.

Prayer takes place at both the individual and communal levels and is similar to Christian prayer, having intensely personal aspects as well as a liturgical dimension during synagogue services. In some ways, the synagogue services resemble Anglican and Roman Catholic services. There probably are ancient links between the way their respective liturgies were compiled. Many synagogues hold daily prayer, although certain types of prayer require a minimum of ten men. Women, at least in traditional synagogues, are kept separate from the men.

Synagogues have three essential elements: the ark, the cabinet where the scrolls of the Torah are stored; the lectern from where worship is led and sermons are preached; and the lamp in front of the ark that burns continually to remind Jews of the ancient menorah that once stood before the ark of the covenant in the temple in Jerusalem. As in many ancient European churches, there also are tablets on which the Ten Commandments are engraved. No images or other artwork of an anthropomorphic nature are allowed in a synagogue.

For practicing Jews, the one shared article of dress is what is known in Hebrew as a *kapah*, or *yarmulke* in Yiddish. This is a small skullcap worn by men during worship as a sign of respect to God. It is also worn in the outside world as a means of witnessing to the wearer's Jewish identity. During communal prayers in Orthodox and most other synagogues, Jewish men wrap themselves in a prayer shawl called a *tallit* that has fringes in accordance with instructions found in the book of Numbers. These fringes are threads with knots in them totaling 613 to symbolize the number of laws identified by rabbinic Judaism as obligatory for all practicing Jews. During certain prayers, Jewish men, and occasionally women, strap a small leather box on one arm and another to the head, centering it on the forehead. These boxes are known as *fefllin* or *phylacteries* and contain four passages from the Torah. This practice is based on Deuteronomy 6:8–9, which commands the Israelites to remember God's commandments: "Tie them as symbols on your hands and bind them on your foreheads. Write them on the doorframes of your houses and on your gates."

Dietary laws play an important role in Judaism. Food that Orthodox Jews may eat is known as kosher food and must be prepared according to strict rules. Today many Jews do not "keep kosher" or do so only within the confines of their homes or on special occasions. To be kosher involves the preparation of not only food and the vessels (the pots and pans) it is prepared in but also the plates and utensils used to eat it. New pots and plates are needed when different types of food are eaten, and to confuse them makes these vessels ritually unclean.

Generally speaking, fruits, vegetables, nuts, gourds, grains, seeds, and fungi may be eaten without restriction except on special occasions. The eating of insects is forbidden, so all plant foods, such as salads, have to be washed carefully to ensure that no insects are mixed up with them. Fish, as the Levitical laws outline, may be eaten provided they have both scales and fins. Eels, shellfish, octopuses, turtles, frogs, and other similar creatures cannot be eaten. The only permissible meats are those that come from animals that chew the cud and have split hooves. This means that while Jews can eat beef, they are not allowed to eat horsemeat, and pork is strictly forbidden. Certain portions of cows such as sinew and blood also are forbidden. All meat must be completely drained of blood. Animals must be slaughtered according to strict, ritually prescribed standards. Dairy products are allowed provided they are kept separate from meat. Birds raised to be eaten, such as chickens, are permitted, but wildfowl are banned. Eggs and similar foods are allowed provided they come from species that are themselves edible, according to Jewish law. What this means is that in practice, Jews who strictly abide by kosher rules cannot eat in most restaurants, are limited in what they can buy from supermarkets, and cannot freely eat food at the homes of non-Jewish or even Jewish friends who do not keep kosher.

These rules, as anthropologist Mary Douglas points out in her classic book *Purity and Danger*, set Jews apart from other peoples.[23] This, Douglas argues, is based on the ancient Hebrew understanding of holiness and the statement in Leviticus 11:45 where God says, "I am the LORD, who brought you up out of Egypt to be your God; therefore be holy, because I am holy." Holiness, Douglas argues, was a physical thing in ancient Israel, and when understood in this way, the Levitical laws, upon which the practice of *kosher* is based, make sense.

The Jewish Family

According to Orthodoxy, the only true Jew is someone born of a Jewish mother. Some groups argue that because of this, it is impossible to convert to Judaism. Most Jews, however, make some allowance for conversion. Within the Jewish household, the circumcision of male children is one of the most important of all events. For Jews, circumcision symbolizes the relationship between God and his people. Circumcision is a religious requirement that must be performed on all male children, although in the nineteenth century some modernizing Jewish groups, especially in Germany, attempted to abolish circumcision as "a barbaric act." Today circumcision has regained its traditional place, and all major Jewish groups as well as sectarian ones practice it. In many synagogues, there is also a ceremony for the naming of girls.

The next milestone in a Jewish man's life is the bar mitzvah, when around the age of twelve or thirteen a boy ritually comes of age. Traditionally there was no similar ceremony for women, but going back to the nineteenth century in Germany, and increasingly popular today, there is also the bat mitzvah for girls. These ceremonies are like super birthday parties that resemble either confirmation or adult baptism as practiced in Christian churches.

The next major milestone is marriage, which traditionally took place at a relatively young age. One interesting aspect of Jewish weddings is that the bridegroom is expected to see the bride before the marriage ceremony, which in most Western cultural traditions is forbidden. After prayers and various other rituals, the rabbi officiating the ceremony gives the couple a glass of wine, which they share. Then the rabbi announces that they are man and wife. At that point the bridegroom throws the glass to the ground and stamps on it.

Although various reasons are given for this act, the most likely one is that it is a reminder of the fragility of life and the fact that even at the happiest moment, suffering may be around the corner. Another explanation is that it is done in remembrance of the destruction of the temple and the hardships suffered by the Jewish people. Whatever the reason, this is one of the unique features of the Jewish wedding.

Finally, at the end of life comes death. Traditionally, Jews are not permitted to leave a dying person alone. As far as possible, family members and mourners are required to stay with the dying person to the end and not avoid the realities of death. Once the person is dead, several rituals take place, including the opening of a window, which some say is to allow the soul to escape the body, while prayers and psalms are recited. For practicing Jews, cremation is prohibited as are autopsies, although on the latter point, there is a certain degree of flexibility. By Jewish law a person ought to be buried in a plain casket and placed in the ground, not in a crypt or mausoleum. The funeral itself should take place as soon as possible after death is confirmed, but not on the Sabbath or a major Jewish holiday. At traditional funerals, mourners tear their garments and cry out aloud to express their grief. Today it is more common for people to wear black as a sign of respect. Another common practice is the placing of a handful of soil from the land of Israel in the casket. Otherwise, most Jewish funerals are little different from any other funeral.

For practicing Jews, the family is the most important social institution and is closely intertwined in their thinking with the Sabbath. Both of these institutions remind Jews of eternal Israel and their relationship to God. The ritual practices associated with the family and the Sabbath are at the heart of Judaism.

Conclusion

With this basic framework in mind, we now turn to the tragic history of Judaism, the rise of anti-Semitism, and the horrors of the Holocaust. Without understanding these, one cannot understand modern Judaism or individual Jews.

chapter twelve

Christians and Jews after the Holocaust

Introduction

Adolf Hitler changed history far more than many people realize. In particular, he changed, perhaps forever, the way Christians and Jews interact and cast a dark cloud over Christian history. To understand Jews and Judaism, this dark history has to be faced.

As a Christian today, witnessing to Jews has become problematic as a result of the Holocaust, which many people see as a result of centuries of anti-Jewish propaganda by Christians. Christians with Jewish friends and acquaintances must tread carefully, and it's helpful to have a solid knowledge of the Holocaust and the complex history of Jews living in Europe. It is also important for Christians to acquaint themselves with the basics of Jewish life and thought to appreciate what it means to be Jewish and the very real trauma experienced within modern Jewish history.

Paul writes in Romans 9–11 that the fate of the Jews is a great mystery. Christians disagree on the fate of future Israel, but we can agree on the importance of understanding them as a people loved by God as well as understanding the way their religion has developed.

Approaching Judaism

Walter Martin's *The Kingdom of the Cults*[1] provides Christians with valuable insight to help them understand Judaism. He writes, "On encountering a cultist then, always remember that you are dealing with a person who is familiar with Christian terminology, and who has carefully redefined it to fit the system of thought he or she now embraces."[2] Replace the word "cultist" with "Christian" and "Christian" with "Jew," and you will begin to understand how many Jews viewed Christians and Christianity even before the Holocaust distorted Jewish-Christian relations further.

Most Christians see Christianity as the fulfilment of the teachings of the *Old Testament,* or Jewish Bible. In our view, Christianity is the natural completion of Judaism, which may leave us puzzled by the fact that Jews do not see things this way.

Jews see the situation very differently. For them Christianity is a systematic distortion of their religion that creates unrecognizable chaos. It is important for Christians to begin their study of Judaism by recognizing that many Jews are genuinely offended by the way Christians approach them. For example, many Christian churches and other organizations hold what they call a "Seder meal" as part of their Easter celebrations. They genuinely believe that in doing so they are reaching out to Jews and honoring their traditions. But for many Jews, the Christian appropriation of the Seder and other practices is an affront that strikes at the root of their being. This is true even though they often recognize that Christians do such things with the best intentions.

As my colleague Professor Eliezer Segal explained to me, "Ask a Christian how important Judaism is to their faith and they have to admit that their religion depends on Jewish texts and interpretations for its ultimate meaning. Ask a Jew how important Christianity is to them and their religion and they will tell you that it is not important at all. Judaism can exist without Christianity, but Christianity is totally dependent on Judaism for its basic frame of reference."

This means that it is particularly important when attempting to explain Judaism to a Christian to carefully distinguish Christian interpretations of Judaism and the religion of Israel from the way Jews see it themselves.[3] That is, to see Judaism as a vibrant religion in its own right. This means seeing Judaism as totally separate from the Christian tradition and not interpreting it through the lens of the *New Testament* or Christian theology.

Another important point when talking to Jews is to recognize that there are many different forms of Judaism in today's world. As a result, Jews belong to an identifiable ethnic group that has elements of both a race and a religion, and many non-religious Jews still practice Jewish rituals on holy days as a means of affirming their identity. Superficially, this looks like the way secular people practice Christmas except that secular Jews who practice Jewish rituals take them far more seriously and usually are very careful to ensure that they do things in the correct way. As Jewish scholar Michael Fishbane puts it, "Judaism is thus the religious expression of the Jewish people from antiquity to the present-day."[4]

Jacob Neusner points out in his book *A Rabbi Talks with Jesus*[5] that Jesus's attitude toward both the family and the Sabbath is totally shocking. The statement of Jesus in Mark 3:35, "Whoever does God's will is my brother and sister and mother," is the antithesis of Jewish thinking. As Neusner observes, "Jesus calls into question the primacy of the family in the priority of my responsibilities, the centrality of the family in the social order."[6] Jesus, he argues, is asking him to "abandon my home and family" for his sake, yet this runs completely counter to the sacred duties conferred on a practicing Jew by the Torah.[7] For Neusner the issue is simply the Torah or Christ,[8] because the teachings of Christ strike at the very heart of eternal Israel.[9]

In Neusner's view, the teachings of Jesus also strike at the other pillar of eternal Israel, the Sabbath. He says, "Like the honor owing to father and mother, therefore the celebration of the Sabbath defines what makes Israel Israel. The entire way of life of the community centers on that day."[10] Clearly, in Neusner's view, Jesus appeared "not to fulfill but to abolish the Sabbath"[11] and by implication the Jewish people as they had existed until his time. For this reason, Neusner cannot accept Jesus's teachings or Christianity.

Few writers have highlighted the differences between Judaism and Christianity as clearly as Neusner. In doing so he also shows Christians, who might otherwise construct a Judaism in the image of their own religion, the fact that Judaism is not simply an earlier, or incomplete, form of Christianity. Rather it is a dynamic religion that should be respected on its own terms and not reinterpreted through a Christian lens. Neusner eloquently sums up Judaism in the following words: "Long ago, far away, God had called a people, a holy, enduring people, into being. God had bound the people to God in a covenant, giving the Torah as terms of that agreement, engraving even into our flesh the very sign of the covenant."[12] This then is the dynamic heart of Judaism.

Recognizing this also means that on many other practical issues, Jews and Christians often take very different views. For example, Rabbi Meir Y. Soloveichik shocked many of his readers when he published an article in *First Things* entitled "The Virtue of Hate," in which he argued that the Jewish tradition rejects the Christian view that promotes love even for one's mortal enemies.[13] When I discussed this with my colleague and friend Eliezer Segal, he admitted that he simply could not understand the Christian view on this issue.[14]

The Road to Emancipation and Integration

The history of modern Judaism has its roots in the Dutch Republic and in the work of authors like Baruch Spinoza (1632–1677), who argued that the essence of religions is ethical systems. Although he was excommunicated by the Jews of Amsterdam, Spinoza's work inspired Jews and non-Jews alike to think anew about the place of Jews in Europe.

In Germany, Moses Mendelssohn (1729–1786), a friend of many German intellectuals in Berlin, the capital city of Prussia, developed Spinoza's ideas to become one of the leading figures of the German Enlightenment. He sought to modernize Jewish life so that Jews would be fully accepted as citizens wherever they lived. His friend Gotthold Ephraim Lessing (1729–1781) reinforced the growing acceptance of Jews with his popular play *Nathan the Wise* (1779), as did the poet Goethe (1749–1832), who could be considered a German equivalent of Shakespeare. Goethe was widely regarded as a "friend of the Jews," and Jews in return promoted his work.

During these years, Jews slowly began to be integrated into the life of European countries. To help formalize this in Prussia, a friend of Mendelssohn who was a military officer, Wilhelm Christian von Dohm (1751–1820), published *Concerning the Amelioration of the Civil Status of the Jews* (1781). This book was enormously influential and helped change the attitudes of educated Europeans toward Jews. Later a wave of emancipation swept continental Europe. As a result, many Jewish scholars argue that it is accurate to see the end of the Jewish Middle Ages beginning in the late eighteenth century, by which time some two million Jews lived in Europe.[15]

In Eastern Europe, the situation was far worse for Jews than in the West. In Russia, Alexander I (1777–1825), after first attempting to expel Jews, changed his policy to one of integration that encouraged the conversion of Jews to Christianity. Not until the later nineteenth century did emancipation get under way, allowing Jews to enter Russian society as full citizens.[16]

The belief that Jews, particularly ones from Eastern Europe who were emigrating to the West, ought to modernize became common, leading to calls by other Jews for them to abandon their traditional dress and mannerisms. Many did. In the 1820s a new Jewish journal, *The First Fruits of the Times,* was published in Vienna to promote the reform of Judaism. This led to a movement that eventually became Reformed Judaism. The movement gave birth to new forms of worship, including hymns, talks modeled on Protestant sermons, and prayers in the vernacular. Worshipers were allowed to worship with their heads uncovered and, in most respects, participate like congregants in a typical Protestant Christian church.

The movement spread to North America, where a small group of Jews in South Carolina introduced reforms that led to an indigenous reform movement first in New York and Baltimore. The initial conference of American Reformed Rabbis took place in Philadelphia in 1869. Four years later the Union of American Hebrew Congregations, the main reform group in America, was founded. Two years later this group established the Hebrew Union College as a center of Reform scholarship and a place to train its leaders.

Back in Germany, reforming movements continued to develop. The most important of these became Conservative Judaism. In many ways it was a compromise between Orthodox Judaism and Reformed Judaism. In New York, the Conservatives founded a theological seminary in 1887. Its most influential leader was Solomon Schechter (1847–1917), a Cambridge-educated scholar who sought a compromise between modern scholarship and traditional practices. Many regard Schechter as "the architect of American Conservative Judaism."

Other scholars, such as Samson Raphael Hirsch (1808–1888), sought to develop a new, invigorated form of Orthodox Judaism that maintained traditional Jewish beliefs and practices while making practical accommodations to the modern world. For him the purpose of life was to serve God in obedience, setting aside questions about personal fulfillment and romanticized spirituality.[17]

Jewish Conversions to Christianity

Before the eighteenth century, Jewish conversions to Christianity were relatively rare. Then as the century progressed, a trickle of Jews became Christians in Western Europe. Early in the nineteenth century, there was a large increase in Jewish conversions, particularly in Germany and the Netherlands.

These converts included two of Moses Mendelssohn's daughters and most of his grandchildren, including the composer Felix Mendelssohn Bartholdy (1809–1847). Other famous converts included David Mendel (1789–1850), better known by his Christian name August Neander, and the jurist Friedrich Julius Stahl (1802–1861), both of whom worked at the University of Berlin. Later, Stahl's writing influenced Dutch Christian leaders Guillaume Groen van Prinsterer (1801–1876) and Abraham Kuyper (1837–1920).[18] While most Christians welcomed these conversions, others, such as the theologian Friedrich Schleiermacher (1768–1834), often referred to as "the father of modern theology," regretted that so many Jews converted to Christianity and attempted to discourage it.

In the Netherlands, the conversion of a number of Jewish intellectuals like Isaac da Costa (1798–1860) and Abraham Capadose (1795–1874) led to a revival of Calvinism and what became known as the Anti-Revolutionary Movement associated with Groen van Prinsterer and Kuyper. Another prominent Jewish convert of this period was Alfred Edersheim (1825–1889), who was converted by a Scottish engineer working in Hungary. He studied at the universities of Edinburgh and Berlin before becoming a Presbyterian minister, missionary to Jews, and prolific writer.[19]

These conversions, and the success of many converts, created a crisis for European and North American Jews, and many Jews claimed that the converts were responding to Christianity for social reasons and opportunities for advancement. Nevertheless, it is hard to deny that da Costa, Edersheim, the Mendelssohns, Neander, and Stahl were deeply moved by Christian teachings and were genuine converts.

The Nightmare of Nazism

It is impossible to know how Christian-Jewish relations would have developed if the First World War had been avoided and the Nazi movement had failed to gain power in Germany. But these things happened, leading to a profound distrust of Christians by many deeply traumatized Jews. Christians need to be aware of what happened and how it has been interpreted.

A key reason for the deep distrust of Christians by Jews, especially American Jews, was British propaganda organized by Lord Vansittart (1881–1957) that claimed Nazi anti-Semitism was rooted in the work of the Protestant Reformer Martin Luther (1483–1546), who also taught absolute obedience to rulers. Vansittart and others argued that it was useless to work with members of the German resistance, such as Dietrich Bonhoeffer (1902–1945), because they were of a divided mind and would never actually assassinate Nazi leaders.[20]

After the Second World War, this idea was popularized by American journalist and former Belin correspondent William L. Shirer (1904–1993), who claimed in his best-selling *The Rise and Fall of the Third Reich* (1960) that "the immense influence" of Luther played a prime role in the birth of Nazism.[21] Although Shirer also recognized the role of neo-paganism in Nazism and Lutheran resistance to Nazis, his comments on these topics were conveniently overlooked and Luther remained the demon.[22]

More recently, in 2003, the idea that Christians were responsible for the Holocaust was popularized by some scholars, such as Richard Steigmann-Gall, in his *Holy Reich: Nazi Conceptions of Christianity, 1919–1945*.[23] That claim is found on numerous websites, such as that of the Freedom from Religion Foundation that specializes in attacking Christianity. As a result, this idea has become widely accepted.[24]

Manfred Gailus and other scholars take a more cautious approach in their work, pointing out the complicity of groups like the so-called "German Christians," without denying the centrality of neo-paganism for core members of the Nazi leadership.[25] Susannah Heschel documents the way the Nazis sought to co-opt theologians who had *Völkisch* (see below) sympathies into studying Judaism with the intent of destroying it by providing them with large research grants and organizing numerous well-funded conferences. This is a tragic story that shows the distortion of Christianity that the Nazis promoted.[26]

It is important to know some German history. Beginning in 1933, the London-based *Friends of Europe* led by the editor of *The Observer* newspaper began to publish a series of seventy-five small booklets on Nazism. What they make clear is that Nazism was perceived as a neo-pagan movement threatening Jews and Christians alike, although it made Jews its first target.

Aurel Kolnai (1900–1973), a Hungarian Jew who converted to Christianity in 1926 after reading the work of G. K. Chesterton (1874–1936), wrote *The War against the West*, which was published in 1938.[27] In it Kolnai clearly showed that the logic of Nazism was both anti-Jewish and anti-Christian because Christianity was seen by the Nazis as a form of Jewish intellectual colonization of other peoples.

A year later, Peter F. Drucker[28] published a telling analysis of the social and intellectual roots of Nazism in his *The End of Economic Man* (1939). He argued that Nazism was a progressive revolutionary movement bent on creating a "new man." Drucker showed that the logic of Nazism necessitated the extermination of the Jews and everything the Nazis saw as tainted with Judaism such as Christianity. He also foresaw the invasion of Russia.

Following the Second World War, the horrors of the Holocaust left Jews stunned and deeply traumatized. The earliest post-war studies of the intellectual basis of Nazism were published by scholars George L. Mosse (1918–1999), Walter Laqueur (1921–2018), Fritz Stern (1926–2016), and others who were Jewish refugees from Nazi Germany. Mosse, Laqueur, and Stern rooted Nazism in the ethos of the earlier German *Völkisch* movement that had rejected Christianity in favor of neo-paganism. This neo-pagan core is brought out well in Peter Longerich's excellent biography *Heinrich Himmler* (2012) and by Karla Poewe in her *New Religions and the Nazis* (2006).[29]

Conclusion

Given the horrific history of modern Judaism and the propaganda making Christians responsible for Nazism, it is important to be well informed on this issue and to recognize the suffering of Jews. Christians who seek to share their faith need to recognize the realities of the Holocaust and how they affect Jewish people. There is, therefore, no simple answer to the issue of evangelism and Jews.

The trauma of the Holocaust makes it very difficult for Jews to seriously consider converting to Christianity. The way they understand the relationship between Christianity and the Holocaust may be incorrect, or at least partly incorrect, but this does not lessen the trauma they have endured. Christians must be sensitive. We need to understand where Jews are coming from and respect their pain.

Our best witness is through living lives that demonstrate the love of Christ and our trust in God. When Jews are open to discussing our faith, we can point them in the direction of fellow Jews who have found peace in Christ, such as German-Jewish historian Frank Eyck, who became a Christian while serving in the British Army during World War II.[30]

chapter thirteen

The Mission of Islam

Introduction

This chapter attempts to present Islam as it is understood by most Muslims. Some Muslims might object at points, but it is an attempt to present a fair account. According to the immensely popular Egyptian Muslim writer Sayyid Qutb (1906–1966), scholarly interpretations such as those found in popular Western books are "the wily attacks of orientalists" who treacherously seek to destroy Islam by reinterpreting its core concepts in secularized Western ways.[1] Qutb is often dismissed as a "sincere extremist" by Western interpreters of Islam, but this overlooks the fact that his works are read throughout the Muslim world and promoted by Muslim organizations in the West. Anyone wanting to understand contemporary Islam needs to take him and other popular Muslim writers, such as Sayyid Abul A'la Mawdudi (1903–1979), seriously.

The Muslim Story

Muslims believe that Islam came into existence with the creation of humanity by God, who is known to Muslims as Allah. After creating the universe, God revealed his will to mankind through the first man, Adam, and demanded obedience. A long line of prophets followed, including Abraham and Jesus. The last and final one was the Prophet Muhammad (c. 570/571–632 AD) to whom God revealed his final will for mankind in the holy Qur'an.[2] Consequently, Muhammad serves as a model and inspiration for all people.

According to tradition, the Prophet Muhammad was a successful businessman living in the oasis town of Mecca, situated at a crossroads between Eastern countries adjoining the Indian Ocean and the Mediterranean world. He received God's call in 610 AD and began preaching the message of the One God. According to Muslim sources, prior to Muhammad's mission, Arabs were a fatalistic people who dismissed ideas about an afterlife, rejected teachings related to a divine judgment, based justice on a system of vengeance and blood feuds, and worshiped hundreds of gods.

Tradition says that Muhammad was a spiritual person who frequently took time off from his daily tasks to meditate and pray. When he was forty years old, during the lunar month of Ramadan, he was meditating in a cave near Mecca when the angel Gabriel appeared to him. This event is known as the "night of power and excellence." Muhammad recited what became the original Surah, or chapter, of the Qur'an, often known as the Recitation. It is Surah 96 of the Qur'an, which Marmaduke Pickthall entitles "The Clot." It begins: "Read: In the name of thy Lord who createth . . ."[3] Here it is important to note that the various chapters, or Surahs, of the Qur'an are not ordered chronologically but, with the notable exception of Surah 1, in terms of their decreasing length.

Muhammad returned to Mecca, where he began preaching and condemning paganism, idolatry, and corruption. Other revelations followed, all centered around the core message that God demands humans to abandon idolatry and worship him alone. The Meccans resisted his call, and increasingly harsh persecutions followed. Eventually, after years of persistence, the people of Medina, which lies two hundred miles north of Mecca, called on Muhammad to mediate in a blood feud that divided their society. Between July and September of the year 622 AD, Muhammad and more than two hundred of his followers moved there. This migration is remembered by the practice of the *Hajj*, or pilgrimage, held annually during the last month of the Islamic year. Today every Muslim is expected to complete a journey to Mecca at least once in their lifetime, making the *Hajj* the largest pilgrimage in the world.

In Medina, Muhammad brought peace, and a revolution in morals and government followed. During this period, various rituals known as the five pillars of Islam were instituted. These are *Shahada*, or the profession of faith; *Salat*, or prayers that must be performed five times a day at fixed hours; *Sawm*, or fasting during daylight hours in the month of Ramadan; *Zakat*, or the giving of alms to the poor; and *Hajj*, the annual Muslim pilgrimage centered on Mecca.

Once his rule was established in Medina, Muhammad turned his attention to Mecca, where the people remained adamantly opposed to his preaching. He initiated a successful guerrilla war and eventually led an army of ten thousand troops and conquered Mecca. After the Meccans surrendered, he showed great leniency, leading many to convert to Islam and accept him as their leader. Then he went on to gain control of the whole of Arabia before dying at the age of sixty-two in June of 632 AD.

Since then Muhammad's example as a successful military and civic leader as well as his personal conduct have served to guide Muslims in their daily lives. Muslims pay close attention to his recorded words and actions as well as to the example of his wives and closest associates, known as his Companions.

After the death of his first wife, Muhammad took a number of other wives. The exact number of his wives is in dispute, but it is usually agreed to be between eight and eleven. Muslims point out that a number of these women were widows of his followers who died in battle for Islam. To devout Muslims, these marriages are a sign of Muhammad's compassion and care for others.

Our knowledge of these events and early Islam generally comes from early biographies of Muhammad[4] and a vast body of literature known as the *Hadith*. The Hadith, which forms the basis for Muslim law and lifestyle, consists of traditions compiled by the immediate followers of Muhammad during his lifetime and after his death. It contains literally thousands of sayings of Muhammad, reports of his actions, and various other details that tell us about his conduct and behavior. The Hadith is regarded as inspired but not direct revelation like the Qur'an. Muslim scholars argue about whether certain parts of the Hadith are genuine and how they ought to be interpreted.

The History of Islam after the Death of Muhammad

Most English-language works on Islam present the Sunni version of Islamic history. While this may be fair, as Sunnis constitute the vast majority of Muslims worldwide, it should be remembered that there are various other Muslim traditions that see things differently. The second largest Muslim tradition worldwide is the Shia, with a radically different interpretation of early Muslim history.[5] The Sunni view is presented here as the basis for our understanding of Islamic history, while Shia differences on some key events are noted.

After the death of Muhammad in 632 AD, his close Companion Abu Bakr (573–634 AD) became the first Caliph, or spiritual and political leader of Islam, in 632 AD. He waged successful wars against rebels and various people claiming to be prophets in their own right. Under his guidance, Muslim armies began an invasion of Syria, which was part of the Christian Byzantine Empire and an important educational center. Abu Bakr ordered the compilation of what was to become the official version of the Qur'an, arranging it in its present order, and the organizing of the collection of the Hadith as well.

Abu Bakr was followed by Umar (579–644 AD) as the next Caliph. Under his rule, Muslim armies conquered Iraq, Iran, Syria,

Palestine, and Egypt. He was assassinated in 644 AD when Uthman (577–656 AD) became Caliph. He too was assassinated, in 656 AD, and was followed by Ali (601–661 AD), Muhammad's adopted son and son-in-law who had married the Prophet's daughter Fatima. Known for his piety and simple way of life, he was a good ruler, a poet, and the first person to write an Arabic grammar.

Ali's Caliphate marked a major turning point in the history of Islam and was marred by two revolts. The first was led by Aisha, the youngest wife of Muhammad and daughter of Abu Bakr. In this revolt, the army of Ali was victorious. Later Mu'awiya (602–680 AD), the Muslim governor of the province of Syria, rebelled against Ali's rule. Ali's army greatly outnumbered that of Mu'awiya, and victory seemed certain, but Ali entered into negotiations and made peace with the rebels. Accounts differ, with some saying Ali's army refused to fight fellow Muslims, while others claim that Ali was a natural peacemaker. Whatever the reason, this act of leniency led to his assassination in 661 AD and the division between Sunni and Shia Islam that continues today.

These early events coincided with the establishment of the Caliphate. A Caliph is a political and social leader in Sunni Islam who governs by military power. The Caliphate is usually subdivided into three periods. From 632 to 661 is the period known as that of the "Right Guided Caliphs." This early period was followed by the Umayyad Empire from 661 to 750, which saw the rapid expansion of Islam as Muslim armies established Islamic rule over North Africa, much of Spain, Persia, large areas of Afghanistan, and most of what is now Pakistan. The Abbasid Empire replaced the Umayyad Empire in 750 AD. It ended with the destruction of the Caliphate by the Mongols in 1258 AD.

The age of the Caliphate was the golden era in Islamic history. After its destruction, numerous rival Muslim rulers vied for power. The Mamluks established a dynasty in Egypt and conquered Syria. Turkish power also grew, leading to the eventual conquest of the

Christian city of Byzantium, modern Istanbul, by the Turks in 1453 and expansion of Islam into eastern Europe.

From the beginning, military victories of Muslim armies were seen as miracles that proved the truth of Islam. These conquests led to the belief that Islam was "spread by the sword." In fact, Muslims often sought to establish their rule over subject peoples without attempting to convert them, because non-Muslims were a major source of taxes for newly established Islamic states. Conversions to Islam generally came much later.

In the sixteenth century, three Muslim empires were established. These were the Safavid Empire in Iran and Persia, which ruled from 1501 to 1736; the Mogul Empire, which ruled in India from 1526 until it was annexed by Britain in 1857; and the Turkish, or Ottoman, Empire that was founded in 1350 and only disintegrated after World War I, leading to the state of modern Turkey that today hovers between secular and Islamic rule. Following World War I, various new states were founded, such as modern Egypt, Saudi Arabia, and Iraq, in former Ottoman provinces.

The Centrality of Muhammad and the Qur'an in Islam

Islam presents a straightforward system of belief and practice. At its core is the declaration, known as the *Shahada*, which must be recited in Arabic. In English translation it states that "there is only one God and Muhammad is His prophet."[6] Every true Muslim recites this in prayer and on numerous other occasions every day. In the Qur'an it is found in separate verses that were later combined into one as can be seen from *Surah*s 37:35 and 48:29. This declaration of faith is engraved on many mosques and other Islamic buildings, including the Dome of the Rock, which was built on the site of the Jewish temple in Jerusalem. Reciting the phrase in the presense of two Muslim witnesses is also the basis of conversion to Islam.

Muslims believe that humans must obey God's law as revealed in the Qur'an and seen in the life and example of Muhammad, recorded in the Hadith.[7] Central to this belief is a distinct view of revelation. From the Muslim viewpoint, Christians confuse the concepts of revelation and inspiration. For Muslims, only the Qur'an is the direct revelation of God.

According to the teachings of Islam, the Qur'an was recited by Muhammad, who sometimes entered a trance-like state to do so. When he recited the Qur'an, his followers, especially those close to him known as his "Companions," wrote down the words he spoke. These were written on anything that came to hand. Sometimes they were written on parchment, sometimes on pieces of bone, and often on palm leaves. During Muhammad's lifetime, these verses were remembered and recited by his followers.

Following Muhammad's death, Abu Bakr, who became the Muslim leader, was worried that the words of the Qur'an might be forgotten once he and the other Companions of Muhammad died. He ordered the collection of as many of these writings as possible, and from them what we know as the Qur'an was compiled.

In arranging the Qur'an, Abu Bakr destroyed any variant readings and organized the text into 114 Surahs, or chapters, that were arranged more or less according to their length and not chronologically. These chapters are poetic in form and, according to Muslims, are the greatest example of poetry in existence. Abu Bakr produced a unified manuscript, unlike the New Testament, in that it contains no book divisions or variant readings. There are no original manuscripts that scholars can examine. Nor can anyone know what differences in interpretation the variants that were destroyed may have contained. The Qur'an in its present form was compiled in a manner that all Muslims accept today. The earliest complete manuscripts of the Qur'an come from the second century of the Muslim era, which is the mid-eighth century AD. There are two earlier manuscripts, each containing approximately two pages of text from the first century of the Muslim era. After this time, most extant texts of the Qur'an come from the tenth century AD.

Because the Qur'an relies on Arabic poetic forms and is believed to be the actual words of God, it cannot be translated into any other language. Muslims must learn the Arabic text to interact with it directly. All so-called translations are more accurately described as renditions that convey the meaning of the Qur'an but are not the Qur'an itself. This is why Marmaduke Pickthall titled his translation *The Meaning of the Glorious Koran*[8] to make it quite clear to the reader that what they were reading was not the Qur'an itself.

In the Qur'an there is a clear distinction between the early, or Medinan, *Surahs* and the later, or Meccan, *Surahs*. In general, we can say that the Medinan *Surahs* are far more inclusive and ecumenical than the later Meccan *Surahs*. The later Meccan *Surahs* are believed to be more authoritative than the earlier *Surahs* whenever there are questions about their teachings. For most Muslims, *Surah* 9 represents the final revelation given to Muhammad and is seen as abrogating all earlier revelations. This is important because *Surah* 9 takes a far more critical view of other religious traditions, including Christianity and Judaism, than the early Medinan *Surahs*.

While the doctrine of abrogation is important for many Muslims, a minority reject it. The doctrine teaches that in revealing the Qur'an, God abrogated, or ruled as no longer applicable, certain early verses that conflicted, or appeared to conflict, with later verses. A good example is the fact that in early Islam, drinking alcohol was apparently allowed, as in *Surah* 2:219. Later, drinking was banned in *Surah* 4:43 and in other places.

Apparent contradictions like this are interpreted by some Muslims as an example of God's progressive revelation in the Qur'an, which abrogates earlier teachings of the Qur'an as needed. Muslims who accept abrogation base the practice on *Surah* 2:106, which reads, "Such of Our revelations as We abrogate or cause to be forgotten, we bring (in place) one better or the like thereof. Knowest thou not that Allah is able to do all things?" Many also believe that *Surah* 9 abrogates all other *Surahs* when there is any doubt about the correct interpretation of the Qur'an.

We must be careful not to overstate Muslim adherence to abrogation. Some Muslims reject it and suggest it was developed by scholars who claimed to be Muslims but either were led astray or were secret enemies. For example, Muhammad Khalifa blames the popularization of the doctrine on modern "Orientalists."[9]

When reading the Qur'an, the context of the verses is not always clear from the text itself because it is poetic and difficult to understand. The meaning of many verses has to be explained from other sources, primarily the Hadith. Although all Muslims accept the importance of the Hadith, not all Muslims accept the same Hadith. Sunni Muslims have the largest Hadith collections and, until recently, few of these were translated into English. The Shia accept a much smaller collection of Hadith, and some Shia authors claim that Sunni Muslims manufactured Hadith during the reigns of the first four Caliphs to discredit the claim that Ali, the son-in-law of the Prophet, was the rightful ruler of the Muslim community.

There are four basic sources of authority in Islam for the development of Islamic Law and interpretation of the Qur'an. The first source of authority and the ultimate authority for interpretation is the Qur'an itself. If at all possible, verses in the Qur'an that appear to be unclear are to be interpreted by other verses in the Qur'an.

The second and major source of interpretation and understanding is the example of Muhammad, whose actions and sayings are recorded in the Hadith. It is from the Hadith that we learn how Muhammad lived and how he interpreted the Qur'an. Since there are thousands if not hundreds of thousands of Hadith, one of the tasks of Muslim scholarship is to determine which Hadith are spurious and which are genuine and can be traced back to Muhammad.

The third major source of interpretation is the consensus of the Muslim scholarly community based on historical precedents and

Muslim practice and opinion in general. Scholarly interpretations of both the Qur'an and the Hadith can be weighed and carefully considered until a conclusion is reached and consensus is arrived at that is agreeable to the community.

The fourth major source of interpretation is analogical argument using deduction and induction based on the other three sources.

Four classical schools of qur'anic interpretation exist. For most Muslims, these schools are authoritative, and there is no room for private interpretations. Muslims must abide by their teachings. Since these schools are complex, we cannot go into a discussion of them here. All one must know is that they settle all the major questions within Islamic theology, life, behavior, and law.[10]

Other Core Beliefs of Islam

The vast majority of Muslim scholars reject Western ideas about the secular state as incompatible with Islam, because they remove morality from public life. Author Sayyid Abul A'la Mawdudi (1903–1979), whose work is promoted by the influential Islamic Foundation in Leicester, England, explains that "the ultimate objective of Islam is to abolish the lordship of man over man and bring him under the rule of the One God."[11] He explains what this means in political terms: "Corrupt rule is the root of all evils you find in the world. Governments have access to power and resources; they frame laws: they control administration, they possess the instruments of coercion like the police and army. Evils exist and flourish in the life of society because governments themselves either spread them or condone them."[12]

Abul A'la Mawdudi argues that "if people are free to commit adultery, no amount of sermons will stop them. But if governments forbid adultery, people will find it easier to give up this evil practice."[13] He writes: "If you really want to root out corruption now so widespread on God's earth, stand up and fight against corrupt rule;

take power and use it on God's behalf. It is useless to think you can change things by preaching alone."[14] Earlier, he made it clear that "to stake everything you have—including your lives—to achieve this purpose is called Jihad. The Prayer, Fasting, Almsgiving, and Pilgrimage, all prepare you for Jihad."[15]

Abul A'la Mawdudi frames jihad as the highest obligation of the Muslim. As he writes, "Merely believing in God as God and in his law as the true law is not enough . . . a sacred duty devolves upon you: wherever you are, in whichever country you live, you must strive to change the wrong basis of government, and seize all powers to rule and make laws from those who do not fear God. . . . The name of this striving is Jihad."[16] To avoid any misunderstanding of his meaning, he goes on to say, "So go forward and fight; dislodge the rebels of God from the government and take over the powers of caliphate. . . . Such a government will quickly be able to reform the people."[17]

The radical nature of such a call for social revolution is made clear when Abul A'la Mawdudi argues for the imposition of Sharia law based on the Qur'an and Hadith because, he says, Muslims cannot live content in a country where secular law prevails. To accept popular sovereignty or the law of existing nations is wrong because one cannot serve two masters. Muslims have to choose to be Muslims and obey God's law revealed in the Qur'an or to disobey God and follow the laws of men.[18]

Some readers may think Mawdudi represents an extreme wing of Islam, but however extreme his views may sound to non-Muslims, they are widely accepted by the majority of Muslims worldwide. There are exceptions, and the Ismaili in particular do not embrace this type of thinking. But most Muslims who take their religion seriously do.

Afif A. Tabbarah (b. 1923), another best-selling Islamic author, writes in his widely read *The Spirit of Islam* that "the Islamic nation is commanded to establish justice on earth. . . . The *Qur'an* demands believers fight in the cause of God."[19] Tabbarah states that "the *Qur'an* uses various means to stimulate people to the war of *Jihad* in the cause of God." Although he notes that most Muslims do not like fighting, he reminds them of *Surah* 2:216 that says, "Warfare is ordained for you, though it is hateful unto you; but it may happen that ye hate a thing which is good for you, and it may happen that ye love a thing which is bad for you. Allah knoweth, ye know not." More recently the Ayatollah Khomeini (1902–1989) spread essentially the same message in his book *Islam and Revolution,*[20] where he argued for the establishment of an Islamic government, presumably worldwide, with *jihad* as one of the means to bring it about.[21]

Popular writer Karen Armstrong and scholar John L. Esposito argue that the real meaning of jihad is struggle, which some present as an entirely personal spiritual exercise, rather than warfare.[22] While struggle is certainly a part of jihad, from the beginning, armed warfare has played a major role in Islam. This can be seen by reading the Qur'an, particularly Surah 9, and by looking at various scholarly studies of *jihad* based on Islamic history and texts.[23]

When Muslims say "Islam is a religion of peace," they are speaking the truth as they understand it. Since the word *Islam* means "submission," or as some translations render it, "surrender," then Islam is a religion of peace provided people accept Islamic rule. This is not quite the same as saying Islam is a peaceful religion or Muslims are pacifists. Within Islam, war has its place to establish Islamic rule.

Islam demands submission and works to ensure that ultimately all people will submit to Islamic rule. Then and only then will a peace exist on earth as a result of Islamic rule. In the meantime, sincere Muslims divide the world into two areas: those free from Muslim control, which are identified as the "realm of war," and the "realm of peace" where people live under Islamic rule and Sharia law.

Nowhere in mainstream Islamic teachings do we find statements like "love your enemies" (Matt 5:44) or "pray for those who persecute you" (Matt 5:44). Nor do we find proclamations like that of the angel at the birth of Christ who "said to them, 'Do not be afraid.

I bring you good news that will cause great joy for all the people,'" followed by the angelic chorus that proclaimed, "Glory to God in the highest heaven, and on earth peace to those on whom his favor rests" (Luke 2:10–14). Finally, it must be recognized that some pacifist movements exist within Islam, particularly in West Africa, but they represent a small minority of Muslims.[24]

Muslim Communities and Sects

The largest Islamic group containing around 85 percent of all Muslims is the Sunni, a name that means "the trodden path," "way," or "practice" of the Prophet. Today Sunni Islam is dominant in Egypt, Indonesia, Turkey, and Pakistan. The most influential subdivision of the Sunni is the Wahhabi, which originated as a reform movement in the eighteenth century led by Muhammad ibn Abd al-Wahhab (1703–1792). At the core of Wahhabi Islam is a call to return to the pure teachings of the Qur'an and the example of the Prophet. Wahhabism is the dominant form of Islam in Saudi Arabia.

Shia Islam is the second largest Muslim community. Shia are the followers of Ali who remained loyal to his children. In 680 AD, war broke out between the Sunni and Shia followers of Ali's son Husayn. The army of Husayn was defeated, and a massacre followed during which direct descendants of the Prophet Muhammad were killed. This event is remembered by the Shia as the "martyrdom" of Husayn.

According to Shia historians, Abu Bakr illegitimately seized control of the Muslim community. They maintain that his successors undermined the legitimate authority of Ali and the Prophet's family. They argue that when Abu Bakr organized the compilation of the Qur'an and the collection of the Hadith, these works were edited to make them favorable to the Sunni viewpoint. While Shia Muslims usually accept Abu Bakr's edition of the Qur'an, they have grave reservations about his Hadith collections and claim that many sayings and deeds of the Prophet were either omitted or fabricated.

Instead of accepting the Caliphate, the Shia developed the idea of Imam. An Imam is a religious leader who assumes religious and political leadership by virtue of piety and scholarship and is a descendant of the Prophet Muhammad through the line of Ali, who was the first Imam. In the course of history, disputes developed among the Shia about who was the legitimate Imam, with the result that today the community is split into several subgroups.

The Ismailis are a distinct branch of Shia Islam and perhaps most adapted to the Western world. Their leader, the Aga Kahn, is regarded as the living Imam of Islam and a direct descendant of Muhammad through Ali. They consider that he is able to reinterpret Muslim teachings for the modern world, and many Ismailis are modern in dress and outlook.

The Kharijite movement, an early Muslim sect, emerged in 657 AD as a radical charismatic group that promoted a strict morality. Over time a moderate branch of the movement, known as the Ibadiyya, or followers of Abd Allah ibn Ibad (d. 708), emerged. It exercised great influence over the development of Islamic states in Tripoli, Zanzibar, Yemen, and Oman. Today it is the official religion in the Sultanate of Oman.

Probably the best known revivalist movements within Islam are Sufi movements that can be found in both Sunni and Shiite Islam. Essentially, Sufis are mystics who blend the obedience demanded by the Qur'an with a loving devotion to God. At the heart of Sufi Islam is a personal quest for spiritual experience and a living relationship with God. Sufis use various techniques to induce hypnotic states through chanting and frenzied dancing. As missionaries they were very successful, forming monastic-like religious orders, normally restricted to males but without celibacy, which is forbidden in the Qur'an. Historically members of Sufi orders were the shock troops of Muslim armies who fearlessly went into battle in mystical states of ecstasy. The intellectual basis for Sufism is found in the work of Muslim philosopher al-Ghazali (1058–1111 AD) and is highly valued by both Sunni and Shia writers. Although essentially orthodox, al-Ghazali's work also provided the basis for numerous heterodox and heretical groups.

Muslim Piety

Muslim piety begins with a confession in Arabic that translates into English as: "There is no God but God, and Muhammad is his Prophet," which is also sometimes rendered, "There is no God but Allah . . ." The declaration is the basis for conversion to Islam. It is whispered in a child's ear at birth, and it is confessed several times daily.

The Islamic calendar begins with the first day of the Hegira, which commemorates the migration of Muhammad and his followers from Mecca to Medina in September of 622 AD and follows the lunar year. A year in the Muslim calendar averages 354 days. According to *Surah* 10:5, the new moon marks the beginning of each month. Differences between the solar and lunar calendars and a ban on inserting a thirteenth month, or a leap year, mean that in the Muslim calendar, months effectively move backward by eleven days each year. The Muslim year contains the following months and holidays:

Months	Religious Holidays
1 Muharram	New Year's Day on the first day of the month.
	The Shia commemorate the 10th day in remembrance of the assassination of Hussein ibn Ali the son-in-law of Muhammad.
2 Safar	
3 Rabi'I.	The Prophet Muhammad's birthday is celebrated on the twelfth of this month in some Muslim countries. These celebrations are discouraged in places like Saudi Arabia.
4 Rabi'II	

Months	Religious Holidays
5 Jamadi I	
6 Jamadi II	
7 Rajab	The twenty-seventh of the month is known as the night of the journey and ascension of Muhammad.
8 Sha'ban	The Night of Repentance, the fourteenth of the month, is important in India and Indonesia.
9 Ramadan	Muslims are required to fast during the hours of daylight throughout the month. The twenty-seventh is the last night of fasting and commemorates the first revelation received by Muhammad. It is a time of special prayer.
10 Shawwal	The first day marks the breaking of the fast of Ramadan. It is known as Eid al-Fitr and is an obligatory feast day like Easter in the Christian calendar.
11 Dhul-Qu'da	
12 Dhul-Hajja	From the first to the tenth of the month is the time of annual pilgrimage when pious Muslims are encouraged to visit Mecca. On the tenth the Feast of Sacrifice, Eid al-Adha, is another great celebration when gifts are exchanged as in the Christian Christmas. The celebration can continue for several days.

Prayer in Islam is similar to prayer found in liturgical Christian traditions such as Anglicanism, Eastern Orthodoxy, and Roman Catholicism. Practicing Muslims are commanded to worship God in ritual prayers five times a day. This practice is known as *salat*, which has the root meeting of "connection" or "contact" between man and God.[25]

The first prayer time occurs when one wakes, officially between the first light of dawn and sunrise. The second occurs between noon and mid-afternoon. The third takes place between mid-afternoon and sunset. The fourth is between sunset and the onset of darkness, and the final prayer is at night before the dawn.

Each time of prayer is preceded by ritual cleansing using a series of carefully prescribed acts intended to separate the worshiper from the profane world. The first of these acts involves physical cleanliness; the worshiper must wash his hands, mouth, nostrils, face and forehead, feet and ankles three times. Then the worshiper dresses appropriately, covering all places of the body that are normally covered. If possible, they also dress in good, or special, clothing to suit the occasion. Then they prepare a place where they can kneel while facing the direction of Mecca. Usually a prayer mat is used, but it can be almost anything that separates the worshiper from the ground beneath. Ritually, this creates a sacred realm. Muslims may pray anywhere except in cemeteries and places used as lavatories, which are considered ritually unclean. Traditionally, men and women pray separately, and menstruating women are not allowed in a mosque as they are ritually unclean.

Once preparations are over, the worshiper performs a series of ritual actions known as *rakahs*. These involve standing, kneeling, standing again, and falling down on one's face while reciting passages from the Qur'an. The words recited at this time are in praise of God, expressing the believer's submission to and adoration of God. As ritual proclamations, these prayers differ from the type of personal prayers found in Christian churches.

Within Islam, personal prayers do exist and are considered supplications, known as *du'a*, addressed to God. Many Muslims pray for help, guidance, and assistance from God and give thanks to God for personal aid. Yet such prayers are closer to folk religion than to the formal expression of Islam. The required prayers of Islam, or daily prayers, form the central practice of all Muslims and are ritual acts of worship rather than expressions of a personal relationship with God.

Whenever a Muslim performs the daily prayers, it is thought best to pray with a group of fellow Muslims. The best place to pray is a mosque.

There worshipers are led in prayer while facing Mecca. Every Friday, prayer in a mosque is obligatory for all healthy Muslim men. Women, the sick, the old and infirm, and travelers are excluded from this requirement, which is practiced with considerable leniency. For example, very bad weather is a valid excuse for not attending Friday prayer. Anyone engaged in work where absence or neglect might cause danger to others is also excused. Those who miss Friday prayer are required to perform four ritual acts similar to a normal noontime prayer.

Muslims do not address God as their loving heavenly Father; such a concept is virtually blasphemous to a pious Muslim. God is the Creator and Preserver, not the Father of individual people. Talking to God in a casual manner would be very strange.

Sayyid Qutb explains the deeper significance of prayer: "Prayer, an act of total submission and dedication to God, epitomizes the entire Islamic outlook on life." Prayer is "an integrated act of worship dedicated completely to the adoration and glorification of God Almighty. The bodily movements of standing (*qiyām*), bowing (*rukū'*) and prostration (*sujūd*), and the recitation of *Qur'anic* verses and other prescribed text. . . . Maintaining this standard in the performance of prayer is a reminder and a fulfillment of the essence and purpose of Islam as a whole."[26] The purposes of prayer, described by Mawdudi as the "Blessings of Prayer," are first to remind Muslims that they "are servants of God" and "every moment" of their lives must be "dedicated to adoring and obeying Him." Second, it is to teach Muslims their duty toward God because "Islam is not a mere matter of doctrinal faith; it is a way of life to be lived in practice. Islam means surrendering to God and fighting against the Kufr [unbeliever] and evil every minute of your lives."[27] Third, prayer promotes "consciousness of God—being in His Presence" to avoid "His punishments."[28] A further benefit of prayer is that it involves reciting verses from the Qur'an. Prayer constantly reminds Muslims of God's law. Finally, because prayer is best performed with other Muslims, it creates a sense of community.[29]

Conclusion

With this overview of Islam, we can now turn to a Christian response to Islam and some of the issues that can and cannot be profitably discussed with Muslims. These topics are discussed in the next chapter.

chapter fourteen

Responding to Islam

Introduction

Writing about Islam is difficult. On the one hand, many authors praise Islam and avoid critical reflection, while on the other hand, there is a deep-seated fear of Islam in Western society that has nothing good to say about Muslims. Both approaches distort the reality and make it difficult for Christians to have Muslim friends or to talk with them about our faith.

Can We Trust the Bible?

One of the first topics that is likely to come up when talking to Muslims is the claim that we cannot trust the Bible. According to Muslims, the Qur'an clearly teaches that after God revealed his will to humans by inspiring his prophets to write the Bible, their writings were corrupted by later authors. Only the Qur'an is reliable as a sacred text.

Fortunately, this topic was taken up by Christian scholar Gordon Nickel in his *Narratives of Tampering in the Earliest Commentaries on the Qur'an*.[1] What he shows is that this widely held Muslim belief began to be accepted only in the tenth century AD as a result of commentaries on the Qur'an written by Muslim scholars in Spain. Before that, Nickel shows, Muslims accepted the Bible as a reliable text.

This is a complex argument but an important one to know about. All the key details can be found in Nickel's more popular work *The Gentle Answer*.[2]

The Issue of Islamophobia

British Muslim leader James Dickie, also known as Yakub Zaki, who taught Islam at Lancaster University, was brutally honest in rejecting what he saw as attempts by Muslim apologists to present a milk-and-water, or pacifist, form of Islam to the West. Instead, he argued, Islam takes seriously the supernatural nature of the universe and recognizes a preordained, God-created natural and social order. War has a legitimate place in Islamic theology, and anyone wanting to understand Islam needs to recognize this.

Dickie argued that Islam is not a pacifist religion similar to that of the Quakers, but neither does it promote war for its own sake. Rather, Islam believes in defensive war while seeking to bring about the rule of God on earth through cultural, intellectual, and military means.

What I learned was that the term *Islamophobia*, as it is aggressively used by some activists, politicians, and scholars, can be a way of avoiding serious discussion. To the extent that it exists, Islamophobia, like many phobias, is often rooted in deep-seated trauma. The historical experience of people whose ancestors were once conquered by Muslim armies and, as in Greece and Hungary, forced to live as second-class citizens in what were once their own countries, or convert to Islam, is traumatic. Yet the Muslims I have known, often as friends, all accepted that conquest has a place in Islam because it allows for the imposition of God's law on a lawless world. They were willing to engage in debate because they believed that once their side of the story was told, people would respect Islam even if they did not agree with it.

Cautions about Witnessing to Muslims

Once you have developed a friendship with a Muslim, you will soon find that they are happy to talk about their religion and ask questions about Christianity. Here a word of caution is needed. Although Muslims like to discuss religious issues, there are some topics they generally see as acceptable and others they regard as blasphemous. It is important to remember that Sharia law carefully defines blasphemy and its punishment. Also remember that many Muslim countries enforce blasphemy laws as part of their civil code. That said, most Muslims I have known are very kind and friendly people who deserve our respect and friendship.

Be careful about what you say and how you say it, because many forms of everyday Christian speech are objectionable to Muslims and thought to verge on blasphemy. This includes things like talking about "God the Father," saying "our Father," and referring to Christ as "the Lord Jesus Christ." It is also very important to speak about Muhammad respectfully because speaking ill of him is regarded as blasphemy by most Muslims. Always ask Muslim friends if they have concerns about such language, and if they do, ask how they would like to discuss Christian and Muslim beliefs.

The Importance of Knowing European History

When talking to a Muslim, it is important to be sensitive to their experience with Christianity and how they understand key issues. For many Muslims today, the Crusades play a role in their thoughts akin to memories of the Holocaust in Judaism. A basic understanding of the historical events surrounding the Crusades is helpful.

Traditionally, Muslims did not view the Crusades as a problem because they saw the final outcome as a great victory for Islam.

Many Islamic books, particularly children's storybooks, praise the deeds of valiant Muslim warriors ousting Christian armies from the Holy Land.[3] More recently, however, post-colonial thought and similar academic currents have caused some Muslims to see the Islamic world as victims of Christian crusaders.[4]

A knowledge of the Crusades is important. Since the Enlightenment, attacks on Christianity by philosopher Voltaire (1694–1778 AD) and historian Edward Gibbon (1737–1794 AD) and others have rewritten the Crusades as primarily a record of conquest and pillage. This distorts reality.

The background to the Crusades is the impact of the rise of Islam on the Mediterranean world and Europe. In 600 AD, strong Christian communities existed all over the Mediterranean world, north into Scotland, as far south as Ethiopia, and as far east as Georgia. There were also Christian communities scattered around the Arabian peninsula, in Persia and India, and as far away as China and Mongolia. This changed beginning in 633 AD when Muslim armies gained control of Arabia. In the next one hundred years, they quickly conquered Syria, Palestine, Egypt, North Africa, and most of Spain. They also entered France. In the east they conquered Persia, reached the Indus Valley, and invaded Buddhist Afghanistan.

These whirlwind conquests were seen by Muslims as a miracle and proof of their divine mission. They marked the beginning of longer and ultimately unsuccessful campaigns to conquer Europe, India, and China. After the initial conquests, Muslim armies on average invaded Europe once every fifty years until the final siege of Vienna as recently as 1683 AD. *The Timetables of History*[5] and the *World Christian Encyclopedia* show the lingering decline of Christian communities in lands conquered by Muslim armies.[6]

Against this background of invasion and conquest, Pope Urban II responded to an appeal for help from the Byzantine emperor Alexius I (1081–1118 AD) to prevent the capture of Constantinople. The First Crusade lasted from 1096 to 1099 and saw the eventual

liberation of Jerusalem from its Arab conquerors. Arab armies coun-
terattacked in 1174. A series of wars and eight more major crusades
followed until 1291, when European powers effectively conceded
defeat. Byzantium and its capital city Constantinople survived for
another 162 years until they were conquered in 1453.

Following the end of the Crusades, the invasions of Europe
resumed. Greece, Hungary, Albania, and Serbia were invaded and
partially occupied for 125 years in Hungary, 321 years in Greece, 327
years in Serbia,[7] and almost 800 years in parts of Spain. Other parts
of Europe, such as Italy, survived conquest but were subject to regular raids by Muslim armies, while Muslim slave ships terrorized the
coasts of Europe until around 1811.[8]

Muslim invasions and slave raids into areas that eventually
became part of Russia began in 1548, and a Muslim army of Tatars
burned down Moscow in 1571.[9] From 1500 to 1700, Crimean Tatars,
who were Muslim, sold more than two million Russians and Ukrai-
nians into slavery. In reaction, rulers Ivan IV the Terrible (1530–
1584) and Catherine II the Great (1729–1796), waged war against
Muslim-controlled territories in Russia where, once conquered, they
allowed or even encouraged a moderate form of Islam to develop.[10]

Overall, this history of invasions and conquest within Europe
explains why many Europeans have a lasting fear of Islam. It is rooted
in the folk memory of conquest and subjugation.

Muslims often respond that there was no compulsion for people
to become Muslims in the conquered areas. This is true, but non-
Muslims were decidedly second-class and known as *dhimmis*, people
with limited legal protection who were not pagans. As such they
were often subjected to harassment.

Once Muslims gained control of an area, they built garrison
towns close to existing towns and cities, taxing Christians and Jews
who were excluded from participating in government and subjected
to numerous laws. In legal disputes, the testimony of Christians
and Jews was outweighed by the testimony of Muslims. A modern

account of what it means to live as a *dhimmi* can be found in the works of the Egyptian Christian writer who uses the pseudonym Bat Ye'or.[11]

Slaves, Sexual Rights, the Treatment of Women, and Unbelievers

Closely related to the issue of *dhimmitude* is that of slavery. A troublesome aspect of Islamic law is that even though it teaches that the freeing of slaves is commendable,[12] and slaves are to be treated with kindness,[13] slavery is acceptable and a natural outcome of war.

As *Surah* 33:50 says: "Prophet, We have made lawful to you the wives to whom you have granted dowries and the slave girls whom God has given you as booty." Taking slaves in war is regarded as a right in Islam, and slaves may be used for sexual pleasure. *Surah* 33:50 speaks of "those whom thy right hand possesseth of those whom Allah hath given thee as spoils of war."

In *Surah* 4:92, we read that in cases of manslaughter, slaves may be exchanged to pay the necessary compensation. This interpretation appears to be supported in the Hadith[14] and in early biographies of the Prophet Muhammad.[15]

The traditional Muslim view of women is problematic for Christians and other non-Muslims. In his popular *The Meaning of the Qur'an*, Mawdudi translates the first line of Surah 4:34 as: "Men are managers of the affairs of women because Allah has made the one superior to the other."[16]

Commenting on this verse, Sayyid Qutb writes:

> The *Qur'an* states that in Islamic society men are required to look after women. . . . It is a simple fact that one party is properly equipped for this role and assigned the duty to play it while the other is not. . . . Moreover, women prefer for the man to assume authority and responsibility for the family.

Many women worry, feel dissatisfied and unhappy, when they live with men who relinquish their role for any reason. Even women who try to challenge the man's role readily admit to this.[17]

In instances where women rebel against their husbands, Qutb suggests three responses based on his reading of the Qur'an. First, "admonish them."[18] If this does not work, refrain from sexual relations. Finally, as a last resort, beat them. This last measure he describes as "a disciplinary measure akin to the punishment a father or a teacher may impose on wayward children."[19] Such instructions appear highly problematic to many, as scholar Mohamed Mahmoud recognizes.[20]

Mahmoud suggests one can get around the command to beat a disobedient wife, but passages in the Hadith where Muhammad appears to say women are inferior to men in their reasoning are difficult to sidestep. For example, the Hadith *Sahih Bukhari*, which is generally regarded as a reliable source, says:

Then he [Muhammad] passed by the women and said, "O women! Give alms, as I have seen that the majority of the dwellers of Hell-fire were you [women]." They asked, "Why is it so, O Allah's Apostle?" He replied, "You curse frequently and are ungrateful to your husbands. I have not seen anyone more deficient in intelligence and religion than you. A cautious sensible man could be led astray by some of you." The women asked, "O Allah's Apostle! What is deficient in our intelligence and religion?" He said, "Is not the evidence of two women equal to the witness of one man?" They replied in the affirmative. He said, "This is the deficiency in her intelligence. Isn't it true that a woman can neither pray nor fast during her menses?" The women replied in the affirmative. He said, "This is the deficiency in her religion."[21]

Suffice it to say that Islam appears to take a different view of women than the view found in the Hebrew Bible and New Testament. The Qur'an also appears to teach that followers of Muhammad are to be "ruthless to the unbelievers but merciful to one another."[22] In another verse, unbelievers are described as the "worst of created beings."[23] How very different these sayings are from the command of Jesus to "love your enemies and pray for those who persecute you."[24]

Conclusion

People often claim that talking about slavery and traditional attitudes to women in Islam is unfair and verges on Islamophobia, because these verses applied only in the past. Yet there is no justification for such a claim. Many respected Islamic authors of currently popular works accept the Qur'an's and Hadith's teachings on slavery and women as realities and discuss their application today.

Slavery continues to exist throughout much of the Muslim world, while a growing number of cases of Muslim-owned slaves have also been reported in Western countries.[25] The grooming scandals that rocked Britain in recent years showed how deeply engrained are some Islamic attitudes toward sex among Muslim men living in the West.[26]

There is no doubt that many Muslims in the West and in traditional Muslim countries are ashamed and outraged by such attitudes and practices.[27] Therefore, while they need to be discussed and Muslims must deal with such attitudes and practices within their own communities, it is important not to appeal to such things and use them as an excuse for intolerance. As Christians we have a duty to show Muslims that we are not bigots but followers of Christ who seek the welfare of all people, whether or not they share our beliefs and faith.

Questions about the significance of historic Islamic teachings today can introduce worthwhile conversations with Muslims.

They can also encourage Christians to reflect on how we live and treat others. As Jesus said in Matthew 7:5, "You hypocrite, first take the plank out of your own eye, and then you will see clearly to remove the speck from your brother's eye." Living up to the teachings of Christ is a challenge facing all Christians, including those who seek to witness to Muslims.

Conclusion

When Jesus sent his disciples into the world, he gave them the Great Commission: "Go and make disciples of all nations, baptizing them in the name of the Father and of the Son and of the Holy Spirit."[1] Christians were commanded to preach "this gospel of the kingdom" in "the whole world." Then, and only then, "the end will come."[2]

Today this obligation to proclaim the gospel remains with us. But there is one big difference between our time and that of earlier ages of evangelism. Since the late eighteenth century, Christians have faced a growing barrage of anti-Christian propaganda. At first this took the form of rationalist attacks on Christian beliefs, the existence of God, and the reliability of the Bible. These attacks then developed psychological and social dimensions that included an appeal to the existence of other religions as an argument against the Christian faith. In the late nineteenth century, Theosophists took things a step further by actively promoting the virtues of other world religions. We now are faced with the twin tasks of defending our faith and proclaiming the gospel.

Many good people live without Christ. As the early church and Christian missionaries always acknowledged, there are "the good pagans" or, in today's terms, members of other religious traditions. Christians have a lot in common with them as fellow citizens in the contemporary world. We have the obligation to share the gospel of Christ with them in ways they can understand and appreciate.

This means we have to understand what they believe and why,

respect them, and not blindly condemn their beliefs and practices while continuing to maintain our own integrity.

It is important to remember what separates Christians and Christianity from other religious traditions and their followers: our God is a personal God, and he created us in his image out of love. This is why doctrines like the Trinity are so important, because they tell us that love, personality, and communication existed in the Godhead before the creation. When people say, "All religions are the same," they are wrong.

Christianity and Yogic Religions

The difference between Christianity and Buddhism is most obvious because of Buddhism's denial of the self, which in Buddhism is "a mere fragment of the imagination."[3] This belief directly contradicts everything we know and experience. Although not stated quite so bluntly, the Hindu tradition, in all of its many forms, takes a similar position. For the Hindu, although the self may be real, it is also illusory and has to be absorbed into a greater whole or be annihilated. For Hindus our world may or may not have some form of "reality," but it is ultimately illusory.

At its core, the Hindu tradition is remarkably similar to Buddhism. Both share the view that the world of experience traps us in the wheel of existence. Nirad C. Chaudhuri, in his book *Hinduism: A Religion to Live By*, explains this in terms of the quests for power and protection.[4] In Hinduism, elite practitioners—gurus and priests—seek power though rituals, incantations, and the control of magical powers. Ordinary Hindus seek protection in everyday life from evil powers through the mediation and assistance of the religious elite.

Both elites and ordinary people live in a world of illusion trapped by the wheel of existence from which the elite hope to eventually escape. Whether this is possible Chaudhuri has his doubts.[5] What is important, he stresses, is the ability of Hinduism to provide ordinary

Hindus with "support in this world," "consolation," and "joy."[6] Hindu beliefs and practices serve to make life bearable and even enjoyable.

He writes, "Religion among the Hindus was never separated from their general life, and . . . sensual enjoyment . . . at the fairs and festivals." He adds that this allowed "men to sell their goods" at fairs where "professional prostitutes" plied their trade. In fact, he adds, "In ancient India, prostitution was interwoven with daily life and religion in what was a very 'democratic' ethos."[7] It was this aspect of the Hindu tradition that Christian missionaries and later Hindu reformers found most objectionable because ritual prostitution exploited women.[8]

From a Christian perspective, both Buddhism and Hinduism fail the test of logical coherence and human experience. There seems to be no certainty in Buddhism or Hinduism that ordinary people, or even religious professionals, will ever escape from the wheel of illusion.[9] The only real difference between the Hindu and Buddhist solutions to the problem of existence is that Hindus stress the importance of making the best of a hopeless situation, while Buddhists face the grim reality.

Both traditions find the cause of suffering in the ontological, or essential, structure of the universe. Christians affirm that creation has a purpose and that God entered history to demonstrate his love to humans.

Christians and Abramic Religions

Islam and Judaism share with Christians the belief in a creator God. But in contrast to Christianity, they usually see God as far more remote, stressing his creative power while downplaying any relationship of love between God and his creation. Islam has many similarities with the Jewish tradition that preceded the revelation of the Qur'an and the preaching of Muhammad. In fact, when Muslim armies first conquered the Christian lands of what today are Egypt and Syria, Christians saw Islam as a form of Judaism.[10]

For Jews and Muslims, the emphasis is on obedience to the law of God. This is commendable, but both religions require an army of scholars to interpret the text of their scriptures, either the Old Testament or Qur'an, for ordinary people. Christianity, even in its Eastern Orthodox and Roman Catholic forms, places far more emphasis on the response of the individual to God's call and the importance of their taking upon themselves the duty of applying biblical teachings to their life. Ministers, priests, elders, and scholars all play a role in this, but essentially the task of deciding how to act is left to the individual, guided by their understanding of the Bible, even if that understanding comes from preaching and pictures when a person is illiterate. This is an enormous difference that separates the Christian view of human duties from that of Judaism and Islam.

Jesus's words in Matthew 12:48–50 play an important, if unrecognized, role in Christian thinking: "'Who is my mother, and who are my brothers?' Pointing to his disciples, he said, 'Here are my mother and my brothers. For whoever does the will of my Father in heaven is my brother and sister and mother.'"

Christians are so familiar with this verse that they often fail to see its revolutionary implications and its effect on society. Judaism, as Jacob Neusner argued, is rooted in family-based genetic relationships.[11] Although Islam proclaims the brotherhood and sisterhood of all Muslims and genuinely attempts to practice this through hospitality, Islam reserves a special place for the descendants of Muhammad.[12] And as Gavin Flood points out, "A Hindu is someone born within an Indian social group, a caste, who adheres to its rules with regard to purity and marriage."[13] Only Buddhism and Christianity break with the idea of genetic descent as religiously important. For both, descent is unimportant and all people are equal. However, in Buddhism, people are only an illusion and do not really exist. It is therefore safe to say that the attitude of Christianity to the individual is unique among the world's religions.

The Way Forward

Early on, Christians developed three successful communication techniques to spread the gospel, which the church embraced with great success. First, they recognized that eventually Jesus would return, but that he clearly said we do not know when this will happen. Christians must take the long view and build for the future.[14]

Christians developed the skills of nurses to help the sick, which despite the skills of ancient doctors was something new and life-changing. They also founded orphanages and hospices to serve both the young and the old. As the great cathedrals of Europe show, they planned for the future by creating institutions and the needed buildings that reached forward to future generations. Some churches and cathedrals took hundreds of years to complete.[15]

Second, they developed a rational case for Christianity based on logical arguments and the presentation of evidence. In the beginning of the Gospel of Luke we read,

> Many have undertaken to draw up an account of the things that have been fulfilled among us, just as they were handed down to us by those who from the first were eyewitnesses and servants of the word. With this in mind, since I myself have carefully investigated everything from the beginning, I too decided to write an orderly account for you, most excellent Theophilus, so that you may know the certainty of the things you have been taught.[16]

From the beginning, Christians argued for the truth of their claims. A survey of Western intellectual history shows that Christians Augustine of Hippo (354–430 AD), the Venerable Bede (672–735), Anselm of Canterbury (1033–1109), Thomas Aquinas (1225–1274), Martin Luther (1483–1546), John Calvin (1509–1564), Jonathan Edwards (1703–1759), Charles Hodge (1823–1886), and Abraham Kuyper (1837–1920) not only were great preachers but were in the forefront of the intellectual life of their day. They took the ideas of their time seriously and interacted with them.

Third, Christians engaged with the society around them as reformers who shaped the lives of millions of people, creating cultures that even their critics admired. In doing so, they sought to change society through gradual reforms. A good example of this is their implicit opposition to slavery, which took centuries before the results began to show.[17] Tragically, slavery returned in the late sixteenth and seventeenth centuries, but once again a Christian antislavery movement developed, which led to abolition of slavery in Europe and the Americas by the end of the nineteenth century.[18]

Unfortunately, following the Reformation, an integrated approach to evangelism was largely forgotten, and Christians began to stress instant conversions. For about five hundred years, the instant approach worked well in societies firmly grounded in the Christian tradition and stories of the Bible. Today this is no longer the case. We need instead to embrace an older, slower form of evangelism. This means taking the long view and making full use of both rational arguments and practical demonstrations of Christian living. We also need to recognize that Christians are the target in a propaganda war intent on destroying the church.

Because many Christians do not know about the past achievements of the church, they are easily intimidated by critics and tend to be ashamed of what they are told Christians did in the past. Churches, for the peace of mind of believers, need to educate their members about their faith as they once did. They need to teach their own children and engage members of other religions. The task before us is daunting, but as the history of the church shows, we as a community have been here before. We must let our light shine before all people so that they see our good deeds and praise God.[19]

Notes

Chapter 1: Welcome Back to the First Century

1. William Barkley, *Commentary on the Acts of the Apostles* (Edinburgh: St. Andrews Press, 1976), 130.
2. F. F. Bruce, *Commentary on the Book of the Acts* (Grand Rapids: Eerdmans, 1983), 348–65.
3. Bede, *The Venerable Bede Commentary on the Acts of the Apostles*, ed. Lawrence T. Martin (Collegeville, MN: Cistercian, 1989), 142. Various older versions of Bede's work are available for download at Internet Archive, https://archive.org/details/texts?and%5B%5D=Venerable+Bede&sin=.
4. Bede, *Venerable Bede*, 144.
5. Bede, *Venerable Bede*, 145.
6. Bede, *Venerable Bede*, 142–43; Bruce, *Acts*, 354–55.
7. Irving Hexham, *Understanding World Religions* (Grand Rapids: Zondervan, 2001).
8. Mark Howell Live, www.markhowelllive.com/understanding-world-religions-new-on-the-next-christians-reading-list/.
9. See Elazar Barkan, *The Retreat of Scientific Racism* (Cambridge: Cambridge University Press, 1992), and Saul Dubow, *Scientific Racism in Modern South Africa* (Cambridge: Cambridge University Press, 1992).
10. Romans 1:19–23.
11. John Shelby Spong, *A New Christianity for a New World* (San Francisco: HarperCollins, 2001).
12. Gretta Vosper, *With or without God* (Toronto: HarperCollins, 2008).
13. Avril A. Powell, *Muslims and Missionaries in Pre-Mutiny India* (London: Curzon, 1993), 232–34, 242–55.
14. In Ananda W. P. Guruge's *From the Living Fountains of Buddhism: Sri Lankan Support to Pioneering Western Orientalists* (Colombo: Ministry of Cultural Affairs, 1984), 339–40. The entire letter is on pp. 337–44.
15. This comment was made to the author by Prof. Edward Conze during a conversation they had in 1968.

Chapter 2: The Experiential Core of Primal Religions

1. John V. Turner, *The Primal Vision: Christian Presence amid African Religion* (London: SCM, 1963); cf. F. B. Welbourn, *Atoms and Ancestors* (London: Edward Arnold, 1968).

2. Pew-Templeton Global Religious Futures Project: http://globalreligious futures.org/regions/sub-saharan-africa/religious_demography#/?affiliations _religion_id=0&affiliations_year=2010.

3. These comments reflect the author's own experience in South Africa and the observations of his wife, anthropologist Karla Poewe, in Namibia and Zambia. What to Westerners often appears to be a confusing religious situation is well illustrated in Martin West's book *Bishops and Prophets in a Black City* (Cape Town, South Africa: David Philip, 1975), and in numerous anthropological studies of religion in Africa and other parts of the world. The interwoven nature of African traditional religions can be seen in essays by African scholars, such as G. C. Oosthuizen, G. C. Hexham, and Irving Hexham, in *Afro-Christian Religion at the Grassroots in Southern Africa* (Lewiston, NY: Edwin Mellen, 1991).

4. Phillip H. Wiebe, *Visons of Jesus* (New York: Oxford University Press, 1977).

5. Friedrich Heiler, *The Gospel of Sadhu Sundar Singh* (1927; Lucknow, India: Lucknow, 1970); Internet Archive, https://archive.org/details/in.ernet. dli.2015.261765. Mrs. Arthur Parker, *Sadhu Sundar Singh: Called of God* (Madras, India: Christian Literature Society for India, 1919), Internet Archive, https://archive.org/details/in.ernet.dli.2015.237537.

6. Janet Hodegson, *Ntsikana's Great Hymn: A Xhosa Expression of Christianity in the early 19th Century Eastern Cape* (Cape Town, South Africa: Centre for African Studies, 1980).

7. Fred and Paddy are not their real names.

8. Various editions of Jonathan Edwards's works are in print. These include his classics *A Faithful Narrative of Surprising Conversions* (1737) and *A Treatise on Religious Affections* (1746) as well as *The Complete Works of President Edwards* (1844). A good starting place to learn about him and his books is Internet Archive: https://archive.org/search.php?query =creator%3A%22Jonathan+Edwards%22&page=2.

Chapter 3: Encountering African Traditional Religions

1. F. B. Welbourn (1912–1986) was taught physics at Makerere University in Uganda, where he also was the Anglican chaplain from 1945 to 1964. He then returned to England, where he became a pioneer of the academic study of African religion and author of the groundbreaking work *East African Rebels: A Study of Some Independent Churches* (London: SCM, 1961).

2. E. E. Evans-Pritchard, *Witchcraft, Oracles, and Magic among the Azande* (New York: Oxford University Press, 1937).

3. Bede, *A History of the English Church and People* (Baltimore: Penguin, 1968), 86–87.

4. Richard Fletcher, *The Barbarian Conversion: From Paganism to Christianity* (Berkeley: University of California Press, 1999).

Chapter 4: Africa's Forgotten Christian Heritage

1. University of Chicago Divinity School, https://divinity.uchicago.edu/ sightings/martin-luther-and-ethiopian-christianity-historical-traces.

2. Ali Mazrui, *The Africans* (London: BBC Publications, 1986).

3. Ronald Segal, *Islam's Black Slaves* (New York: Farrar, Straus & Giroux, 2001), 55–65.

4. See Segal, *Islam's Black Slaves*.

5. Richard Gray, *Black Christians and White Missionaries* (New Haven: Yale University Press, 1990).

6. For a good discussion of Christian involvement in the anti-slavery movement see Rodney Stark, *For the Glory of God* (Princeton: Princeton University Press, 2003), 291–365.

7. Frank M. Snowden, "Attitudes towards Blacks in the Greek and Roman World," in Edwin M. Yamauchi, *Africa and Africans in Antiquity* (East Lansing: Michigan State University Press, 2001), 246–75.

8. Hans Werner Debrunner, *Presence and Prestige: Africans in Europe. A History of Africans in Europe Before 1918* (Basel: Basler Afrika Bibliographien, 1979), 107.

9. Debrunner, *Presence and Prestige*, 35–36; Graham W. Irwin, *Africans Abroad: A Documentary History of the Black Diaspora in Asia, Latin America, and the Caribbean during the Age of Slavery* (New York: Columbia University Press, 1977), 34–35.

10. George L. Mosse, *Toward the Final Solution: A History of European Racism* (New York: Howard Fertig, 1978), 1–7, 19–20.

11. Voltaire, *The Works of Voltaire: A Contemporary Version*, trans. William F. Fleming, 43 vols. (London: E. R. DuMont, 1901), 34:240. A fuller discussion of this with citations is found in my *Understanding World Religions* (Grand Rapids: Zondervan, 2011).

12. David Hume, *Essays* (London: Routledge, 1906), 152.

13. Georg Wilhelm Friedrich Hegel, *The Philosophy of History*, trans. J. Sibree (New York: Dover, 1956), 99.

14. For examples of the type of debate that raged during the nineteenth century between missionaries and anthropologists who considered themselves the representatives of modern science, see *The Anthropological Review*, vol.

2 (London: Trübmer, 1864). A detailed attack on the missionary claim that Africans are found in the same journal is in vol. 3 (1865). Cf. Saul Dubow, *Scientific Racism in Modern South Africa* (Cambridge: Cambridge University Press, 1995); Elazar Barkan, *The Retreat of Scientific Racism* (Cambridge: Cambridge University Press, 1992).

15. Irving Hexham, "Violating Missionary Culture: The Tyranny of Theory and the Ethics of Historical Research," in Ulrich van der Heyden and Jürgen Becher, eds., *Mission und Gewalt* (Stuttgart: Franz Steiner, 2000), 193–206.

16. World Jewish Congress, www.worldjewishcongress.org/en/news/lemba-tribe-in-southern-africa-has-jewish-roots-genetic-tests-reveal.

17. A. B. Spurdle and T. Jenkins, "The Origins of the Lemba "Black Jews" of Southern Africa: Evidence from P12F2 and Other Y-Chromosome Markers," *American Journal of Human Genetics* 59.5 (1996): 1126–33. See also Mark G. Thomas, Tudor Parfitt, Deborah A. Weiss, Karl Skorecki, James F. Wilson, Magdel le Roux, Neil Bradman, and David B. Goldstein, "Y Chromosomes Traveling South: The Cohen Modal Haplotype and the Origins of the Lemba—the "Black Jews of Southern Africa," *American Journal of Human Genetics* 66.2 (2000): 674–86.

18. Karla Poewe, ed., *Charismatic Christianity as a Global Culture* (Columbia, SC: University of South Carolina Press, 1994), 1–29, 50–69, 234–58.

Chapter 5: The Essence of Yogic Religions

1. A. C. Bhaktivedanta Swami Prabhupada, *The Search for Liberation* (Los Angeles: Bhaktivedanta Book Trust, 1982), 10.

2. Edward Conze, *Buddhism: Its Essence and Development* (Oxford: Bruno Cassirer, 1957), 22.

3. Mircea Eliade, *Yoga Immortality and Freedom* (London: Routledge & Kegan Paul, 1969), 35.

4. The term "Abramic" is used because in Genesis 12–16 we read how God called Abram to follow him. Then in Genesis 17, Abram enters into a covenant with God that involves his name changing to Abraham, who is the father of the Jewish people. Abramic indicates the pre-Jewish call of God that Muslims and Christians can look back to as the foundation of their faith. Muslims reject the later covenant with Abraham, while Christians say it is superseded by the new covenant discussed in Romans 3–5 and the book of Hebrews.

5. Ninian Smart, *Religious Experience of Mankind* (New York: Scribner's, 1969), 70.

6. *Bhagavad Gita*, trans. A. C. Bhaktivedanta Swami Prabhupada (New York: Macmillan, 1968), xix.

7. For a discussion of Western attitudes to Buddhism, see Christmas

Humphries, *Sixty Years of Buddhists in Britain* (London: Buddhist Society, 1968), and Charles Prebish, *American Buddhism* (Belmont, CA: Duxbury, 1979). For a more controversial and entertaining personal account, see the autobiography of Edward Conze, *The Memoirs of a Modern Gnostic*, 2 vols. (Sherborne, England: Samizdat, 1979).

8. Eliade, *Yoga*, 4.
9. Ninian Smart, *Doctrine and Argument in Indian Philosophy* (London: George Allen and Unwin, 1969), 97–105.
10. Smart, *Indian Philosophy*, 107, 114.
11. Eliade, *Yoga*, 14.
12. Peter Brent, *Godmen of India* (Harmondsworth: Penguin, 1973).
13. J. W. Hanson, ed., *The World's Congress of Religions: The Addresses and Papers* (Chicago: Mammoth, 1894), Internet Archive, https://archive.org/details/worldscongressof00worl.
14. Hanson, *Religions*, 366–76.
15. Hanson, *Religions*, 377–87.
16. S. Basu, *Religious Revivalism as Nationalist Discourse: Swami Vivekananda and New Hinduism in Nineteenth-Century Bengal* (New York: Oxford University Press, 2002); David L. McMahan, *The Making of Buddhist Modernism* (New York: Oxford University Press, 2009).
17. Richard Hittleman, *Guide to Yoga Meditation* (New York: Bantam, 1969), 9–14.
18. Mark Singleton, *Yoga Body: The Origins of Modern Posture Practice* (New York: Oxford University Press, 2010), 7–8.

Chapter 6: The Way of the Buddha

1. Ninian Smart, *The Religious Experience of Mankind* (New York: Scribner's, 1969), 70. Here Smart is using the term "men" in the traditional English sense of "humans" or "people."
2. Conze, *Buddhism*, 105.

Chapter 7: The Nothingness of Buddhism

1. Tucker N. Callaway, *Zen Way: Jesus Way* (Tokyo: Tuttle, 1976).
2. Edward Conze, *Buddhism: Its Essence and Development* (Oxford: Bruno Cassirer, 1957), 40.
3. Edward John Carnell, *An Introduction to Christian Apologetics: A Philosophic Defense of the Trinitarian-Theistic Faith* (Grand Rapids: Eerdmans, 1948).
4. Conze, *Buddhism*.
5. Conze, *Buddhism*, 13–14.
6. See, for example, Brian Daizen Victoria, "Engaged Buddhism: A Skeleton in the Closet," *Journal of Global Buddhism* 2 (2001): 72–91.

7. Brian Daizen Victoria, *Zen at War* (Lanhan, MD: Rowman & Littlefield, 2006).

8. See Karla Poewe, *New Religions and the Nazis* (New York: Routledge, 2006).

9. Paul Williams, *The Unexpected Way: On Converting from Buddhism to Catholicism* (Edinburgh: T&T Clark, 2002).

Chapter 8: The Bewildering Complexity of Hinduism

1. Although it is popular for Western scholars to deny the power of the caste system, my experience is that many Hindu students strongly object and argue that it is alive and well even though they themselves no longer believe that it ought to be accepted. The one exception to the survival of the caste system appears to be South Africa, where the one beneficial effect of apartheid was that it caused the Hindu community to forget their caste origins.

2. For a more complex discussion of the idea of ritual purity, readers are generally referred to Roman Catholic anthropologist Mary Douglas's *Purity and Danger: An Analysis of Concepts of Pollution and Taboo* (London: Routledge & Kegan Paul, 1966).

Chapter 9: The Enigma of Hinduism

1. Nirad C. Chaudhuri, *Hinduism: A Religion to Live By* (Oxford: Oxford India, 1997), first published in India in 1979.

2. See "Developing a Christian Response to Buddhism" in chapter 7.

3. Chaudhuri, *Hinduism*, 31. His discussion of history is a long one found on pages 27–63.

4. Kenneth Ingham, *Reformers in India, 1793–1833: An Account of the Work of Christian Missionaries on Behalf of Social Reform* (New York: Octagon, 1973).

5. See Anuja Jaiswal, "Human Sacrifice: 4 Men Kill Youth to Realise Their 'Millionaire' Dream," *The Times of India*, April 15, 2018, https://timesofindia.indiatimes.com/city/agra/human-sacrifice-4-men-kill-youth-to-become-millionaire/articleshow/63773978.cms. See also Puja Changoiwala, "India's Killer 'Godmen' and Their Sacrificial Children," *This Week in Asia*, April 14, 2018, *South China Morning Post*, www.scmp.com/week-asia/society/article/2141250/indias-killer-godmen-and-their-sacrificial-children. See also *BBC News*, "India Child Killed in 'Human Sacrifice Ritual,'" October 1, 2015, www.bbc.com/news/world-asia-india-34409637. For an older but well-documented academic study of this and the impact of Christian missions on India, see Ingham, *Reformers in India*.

6. This raises the possibility that the rise of Hinduism in anything like a systematic form was actually a reaction to Christian missions by members of

ill-defined local religions that had many of the features that later came to be recognized as Hinduism. In fact, some Indian Christians, such as Professor M. M. Ninan in his *The Emergence of Hinduism from Christianity* (San Jose, CA: Global, 2006), claim that in the first few centuries of the Christian era, missions spread Christianity throughout India, creating a reaction that became what we know as Hinduism. Although this claim is interesting, he fails to provide references supporting his ideas, which apparently are largely accepted as "folk knowledge" among many Indian Christians. The suggestion offers an interesting line of investigation that ought to be pursued in the future.

Chapter 10: The Abramic Tradition

1. Irving Hexham, *Understanding World Religions* (Grand Rapids: Zondervan, 2011).
2. B. B. Warfield, *Inspiration and Revelation of the Bible* (Phillipsburg, NJ: P&R, 1951), 131.
3. Genesis 12–24 and Hebrews 11:8–19.
4. Colossians 2:8, 16.
5. See Acts 10; 15:1–29; Galatians 2–4; 1 Timothy 1:4.
6. A good and relatively brief example of this is found in the translated extracts from the writings of the Ayatollah Khomeini edited by Clive Irving and issued as *The Little Green Book: Sayings of the Ayatollah Khomeini* (New York: Bantam, 1980).
7. For a discussion of the importance of metonym, see Karla Poewe, "The Charismatic Movement and Augustine: The Challenge of Symbolic Thought in the Modern World," *PNEUMA: The Journal for the Society of Pentecostal Studies* 11.2 (1999): 21–35, and "On the Metonymic Structure of Religious Experiences: The Example of Charismatic Christianity," *Cultural Dynamics* 2.4 (1989): 361–80.

Chapter 11: The Travails of Judaism

1. Eliezer Segal, *Introducing Judaism* (London: Routledge, 2009), 26–27; Lancelot Brenton, *The Septuagint with Apocrypha: Greek and English* (Peabody, MA: Hendrickson, 2003), preface.
2. So great was the influence of Greek rulers on the Jews who prospered in cities like Alexandria that many abandoned the languages of Hebrew and Aramaic for Greek. Consequently, around 260 BC, seventy Jewish scholars in Alexandria translated the Hebrew Bible into Greek in a translation known as the Septuagint.
3. Today Jews remember this by celebrating the festival of Hanukkah.

4. Alexander Fuks, "Aspects of the Jewish Revolt in AD 115–117," *Journal of Roman Studies* 51 (1961): 98–104.

5. Fuks, "Jewish Revolt," 99.

6. Michael Fishbane, *Judaism* (San Francisco: Harper, 1987), 49.

7. Fishbane, *Judaism*, 51.

8. Fishbane, *Judaism*, 51.

9. Leo Trepp, *Judaism: Development and Life* (Belmont, CA: Wadsworth, 1982), 60–66.

10. Trepp, *Judaism*, 66–75.

11. Information on Jewish demographics can be found on the Central Bureau of Statistics website for the State of Israel at www.cbs.gov.il/he/pages/default. aspx.

12. A translation of this in three volumes is available from Internet Archive, https://archive.org/details/texts?and%5B%5D=Maimonides&sin=.

13. This is also available from Internet Archive, https://archive.org/details/ texts?and%5B%5D=Maimonides&sin=.

14. Rabbi Shmuley Boteach, *The Wolf Shall Lie with the Lamb* (Montvale, NJ: Jason Aronson).

15. Trepp, *Judaism*, 62–64.

16. A selection of his works, mainly in German, can be found at Internet Archive, https://archive.org/details/texts?and%5B%5D=Moses+Mendels sohn&sin=.

17. Trepp, *Judaism*, 94–95; Dan Cohn-Sherbok, *Judaism: History, Belief, and Practice* (London: Routledge, 2003), 253–54.

18. Works about and by him can be found at Internet Archive, https://archive. org/details/texts?and%5B%5D=Felix+Mendelssohn&sin=.

19. See Ezekiel 1:1–28.

20. Cohn-Sherbok, *Judaism*, 220–23.

21. Cohn-Sherbok, *Judaism*, 233–37, 333.

22. A good discussion of Jewish piety and the issues discussed in this and the following sections is found in Stephen J. Einstein and Lydia Kukoff, *Every Person's Guide to Judaism* (New York: UAHC Press, 1989). Eliezer Segal's various popular writings on Judaism are an excellent introduction to popular Judaism and religious practices. They include *Why Didn't I Learn This in Hebrew School?: Excursions through the Jewish Past and Present* (Northvale, NJ: Jason Aronson, 1999); *Holidays, History, and Halakhah* (Northvale, NJ: Jason Aronson, 2000); and *Ask Now of the Days That Are Past* (Calgary: University of Calgary Press, 2005).

23. Mary Douglas, *Purity and Danger: An Analysis of Concepts of Pollution and Taboo* (London: Routledge & Kegan Paul, 1966).

Chapter 12: Christians and Jews after the Holocaust

1. Walter Martin, *The Kingdom of the Cults* (Minneapolis: Bethany Fellowship, 1976).

2. Martin, *Kingdom of the Cults*, 20.

3. A good overview of the Jewish perspective on their beliefs and history is provided by Michael Fishbane in his *Judaism* (San Francisco: Harper, 1987). For a more complex account, see Dan Cohn-Sherbok, *Judaism: History, Belief, and Practice* (London: Routledge, 2003).

4. Fishbane, *Judaism*, 12.

5. Jacob Neusner, *A Rabbi Talks with Jesus* (Montreal and Kingston: McGill-Queen's University Press, 2001).

6. Neusner, *Jesus*, 58.

7. Neusner, *Jesus*, 60.

8. Neusner, *Jesus*, 64.

9. Neusner, *Jesus*, 54.

10. Neusner, *Jesus*, 78.

11. Neusner, *Jesus*, 84.

12. Neusner, *Jesus*, 157.

13. Rabbi Meir Y. Soloveichik, "The Virtue of Hate," *First Things*, February 2003, www.firstthings.com/article/2003/02/the-virtue-of-hate.

14. For further, nuanced discussion see "The Virtue of Hate and the Chief Rabbi," *Chakira*, July 12, 2012, https://chakira.org/2012/07/12/the-virtue-of-hate-and-the-chief-rabbi/.

15. For further reading related to this and the following sections, see Paul Johnson, *A History of the Jews* (London: Weidenfeld and Nicolson, 1987); Howard Morley Sachar, *The Course of Modern Jewish History* (New York: Dell, 1977); and David Rudawsky, *Modern Jewish Religious Movements* (New York: Behrman, 1979).

16. Cecil Roth, *History of the Jews* (New York: Shocken, 1963), 327–46.

17. Johnson, *History of the Jews*, 311–421.

18. Surprisingly, little has been written on this topic. One of the few recent books on this topic is Deborah Sadie Hertz, *How Jews Became Germans: The History of Conversion and Assimilation in Berlin* (New Haven: Yale University Press, 2007).

19. His most famous book is *The Life and Times of Jesus the Messiah* (1883), which remarkably is still in print and use today. His works can be found at Internet Archive, https://archive.org/details/texts?and%5B%5D=Alfred+Edersheim&sin=.

20. For a full discussion of this issue, see Uwe Siemon-Netto, *The Fabricated Luther: Refuting Nazi Connections and Other Modern Myths* (St. Louis:

Concordia, 2007); cf. John Warwick Montgomery, ed., *In Defense of Martin Luther* (Milwaukee: Northwestern, 1970); and Lowell C. Green, *Lutherans against Hitler: The Untold Story* (St. Louis: Concordia, 2007). In fact, Lutherans participated in several bomb plots to kill Hitler that failed largely because they were not given the support they begged for from Britain.

21. William L. Shirer, *The Rise and Fall of the Third Reich: A History of Nazi Germany* (New York: Simon & Schuster, 1960), 91–92, 235–37.

22. Shirer, *Third Reich*, 238–40.

23. Richard Steigmann-Gall, *The Holy Reich: Nazi Conceptions of Christianity, 1919–1945* (Cambridge: Cambridge University Press, 2003), 3–12. For various criticisms of Steigmann-Gall's work, see *Journal of Contemporary History* 42.1.

24. A search of the Freedom from Religion Foundation website will reveal numerous articles associating Christians with Nazism and the Holocaust, e.g., https://ffrf.org/about/getting-acquainted/item/16920-religion-and-the-holocaust.

25. Manfred Gailus and Wolfgang Krogel, eds., *Von der babylonischen Gefangenschaft der Kirche im Nationalen* (Berlin: Wichern Verlage, 2006).

26. Susannah Heschel, *The Aryan Jesus: Christian Theologians and the Bible in Nazi Germany* (Princeton: Princeton University Press, 2008).

27. Aurel Kolnai, *The War against the West* (London: Victor Gollancz, 1938). Although accurate in its depiction of Nazism, the book was published as a popular work by Victor Gollancz and unfortunately lacked academic references despite its copious quotations.

28. Peter Drucker grew up in an Austrian Jewish family that had converted to Christianity.

29. Peter Longerich, *Heinrich Himmler* (Oxford: Oxford University Press, 2012); Karla Poewe, *New Religions and the Nazis* (Oxford: Routledge, 2006).

30. F. Eyck and R. Eyck, *A Historian's Pilgrimage: Memoirs and Reflections* (Calgary: Detselig, 2009). Republished as an e-book by Vogelstein Press, Calgary, 2016.

Chapter 13: The Mission of Islam

1. Sayyid Qutb, *Milestones* (Beirut: Holy Koran, 1980), 12.

2. Sometimes translated as "Koran" in English.

3. All qur'anic citations are from Marmaduke Pickthall's (1875–1936) rendition of the Qur'an entitled *The Meaning of the Glorious Koran: An Explanatory Translation* (New York: Dorset, n.d.; first published in Karachi around 1900). This rendition is used because many Muslim scholars, like my teacher Dr. James Dickie (Jakub, or Yakub, Zaki), claim it is the best. Here

it is important to note that the Qur'an was recited in Arabic by Muhammad and, according to Islamic theology, cannot be translated into another language. All one can do is render its meaning into English and not claim it is a definitive translation because translations lose some of the original meaning.

4. The earliest of these biographies is Rizwi Faizer, ed., *The Life of Muhammad: Al-Waqidi's Kitab al-Maghazi*, trans. Amal Ismail and Abdul Kader Tayob (Milton Park, NY: Routledge, 2011).

5. One of the few history books written in English from a Shia viewpoint is Sayed A. A. Razwy, *A Restatement of the History of Islam and Muslims* (Stanmore, Middlesex: Islamic Centre, World Federation of KSI Muslim Communities, 1997).

6. The exact wording of the *Shahada* is different in various English translations. In recent years the one used here has become the most common translation used in popular explanations of how an English-speaking person can convert to Islam. See section 4 of the website "How to Become a Muslim" at www.wikihow.com/Become-a-Muslim; section 3 of the website "The Religion of Islam: How to Convert to Islam" at www.islamreligion.com/articles/204/how-to-convert-to-islam-and-become-muslim/. It is also found in slightly different words on the BBC Religions website at www.bbc.co.uk/religion/religions/islam/conversion/beginner_1.shtml.

7. The best short introduction to the Qur'an and its interpretation is probably Michael Cook, *The Koran: A Very Short Introduction* (Oxford: Oxford University Press, 2000).

8. Mohammed Marmaduke Pickthall, *The Meaning of the Glorious Koran* (New York: Mentor Religious Classics, n.d.).

9. Muhammad Khalifa, *The Sublime Qur'ān and Orientalism* (London: Longman, 1983).

10. These are the Shafites founded by al-Shafir (767–820 AD), which was historically the most influential school of interpretation. The Hanafite school was founded in Iran in the eighth century and named after Abu Hanafa (699–767 AD). It allows greater scope for personal interpretation and is relatively liberal. The Malikite school, founded in Mecca by Malik ibn Anas (711–795 AD), promotes what is probably an authentic Meccan interpretation of the Qur'an. Finally, there is the Hanbalite school founded by Ahmad ibn Hanbal (780–855 AD), which presents a highly literal and legalistic understanding of the Qur'an. This last school is seen as a forerunner of the Wahhabi interpreation of Islam that is promoted by Saudi Arabia today.

11. Sayyid Abul A'la Mawdudi, *Let Us Be Muslims* (Leicester: Islamic Foundation, 1991), 285. This book was first published in 1985 by the Islamic

Foundation as a text for British Muslims (Mawdudi, 1991), 13–15. As explained in the introduction, it was an updated English-language version of his *Khutubat* originally published in India in 1940. Since then it has been published in various formats and editions and originally appeared in an English translation as *The Fundamentals of Islam* (Lahore: Islamic Publications, 1975).

12. Mawdudi, *Let Us Be Muslims*, 286.

13. Mawdudi, *Let Us Be Muslims*, 287.

14. Mawdudi, *Let Us Be Muslims*, 288.

15. Mawdudi, *Let Us Be Muslims*, 285.

16. Mawdudi, *Let Us Be Muslims*, 290.

17. Mawdudi, *Let Us Be Muslims*, 292–93.

18. Mawdudi, *Let Us Be Muslims*, 295–303.

19. Afif A. Tabbarah, *The Spirit of Islam* (Beirut: Dar El-Ilm Lilmalayin, 1993), 282.

20. Ayatola Khomeini, *Islam and Revolution* (Berkeley, CA: Mizan, 1981).

21. Khomeini, *Islam and Revolution*, 40–149.

22. Karen Armstrong, *Islam* (New York: Modern Library Edition, 2000), 168–75; John L. Esposito, Darrell J. Fasching, and Todd Lewis, *World Religions Today* (New York: Oxford University Press, 2002), 213. Ironically, reference to jihad as a spiritual struggle appears to have been popularized through the publication of Maulana Muhammad Ali's (1874–1951) *A Manual of Hadith* (Islamabad, Pakistan: Ahmadiyya Anjuman Ishaat Islam, 1944), 252–53, and is not to be found in any of the standard collections of the Hadith. Ali was an Ahmadiyya Muslim whose version of Islam is not recognized by many Muslims and in states like Pakistan is officially declared a "non-Muslim" faith. This work, which contains only 690 of the thousands of different Hadith, has been accepted as the standard reference source by many scholars. It is available from Internet Archive, https://archive.org/details/in.ernet .dli.2015.489009.

23. See Rudolph Peters, *Jihad in Classical and Modern Islam: A Reader* (Princeton: Markus Wiener, 1996); Reuven Firestone, *Jihād: The Origins of Holy War in Islam* (New York: Oxford University Press, 1999), 16–17.

24. Authors such as Maulana Wahiduddin Khan, who wrote *Islam Rediscovered: Discovering Islam from Its Original Sources* (New Delhi: Goodword, 2001), belong to this school of thought.

25. The Islamic Supreme Council of America has a useful website that discusses prayer: www.islamicsupremecouncil.org/understanding-islam/legal-rulings/53-ritual-prayer-its-meaning-and-manner.html.

26. Sayyid Qutb, *In the Shade of the Qur'ān*, trans. and ed. Adil Salahi and Ashur Shamis (Leicester: Islamic Foundation, 1999), 222–23.

27. Mawdudi, *Let Us Be Muslims*, 148–49.

28. Mawdudi, *Let Us Be Muslims*, 148

29. Mawdudi, *Let Us Be Muslims*, 150–51.

Chapter 14: Responding to Islam

1. Gordon Nickel, *Narratives of Tampering in the Earliest Commentaries on the Qur'an* (Leiden: Brill, 2011).

2. Gordon Nickel, *The Gentle Answer to the Muslim Accusation of Biblical Falsification* (Calgary: Bruton Gate, 2014). His website, Gentle Answer, is well worth a visit: www.gentleanswer.com.

3. See Shahnaz Husain, *Muslim Heroes of the Crusades* (London: Aa-Ha, 1998).

4. For a discussion of these topics, which were popularized by Edward Said, see Robert Irwin, *For Lust of Knowing: The Orientalists and Their Enemies* (London: Penguin, 2007), and Ibn Warraq, *Defending the West: A Critique of Edward Said's Orientalism* (Amherst, NY: Prometheus, 2007).

5. Bernard Grun, *The Timetables of History* (New York: Simon & Schuster, 1975).

6. David B. Barrett, *World Christian Encyclopaedia* (Oxford: Oxford University Press, 1982).

7. The liberation of Serbia was a slow process that began with a series of revolts in the early nineteenth century that led to de facto independence in 1830, although full independence was not officially recognized until 1878.

8. R. Davis, *Christian Slaves, Muslim Masters: White Slavery in the Mediterranean, the Barbary Coast, and Italy, 1500–1800* (London: Palgrave, 2004); Giles Milton, *White Gold: The Extraordinary Story of Thomas Pellow and Islam's One Million White Slaves* (New York: Farrar, Straus & Giroux, 2005).

9. Alan Fisher, "Muscovy and the Black Sea Slave Trade," *Canadian American Slavic Studies* 6 (1972): 575–94.

10. Cf. Brian Glyn Williams, *The Sultan's Raiders: The Military Role of the Crimean Tatars in the Ottoman Empire* (Washington, DC: Jamestown Foundation, 2013); Geza David Pal Fordor, *Ransom Slavery along the Ottoman Borders* (Leiden: Brill, 2007).

11. Bat Ye'or, *The Dhimmi: Jews and Christians under Islam* (Madison, NJ: Fairleigh Dickinson University Press, 1985); *Islam and Dhimmitude: Where Civilizations Collide* (Madison, NJ: Fairleigh Dickinson University Press; Teaneck, NJ: Associated University Press, 2002); Andrew G. Bostom, *The Legacy of Jihad: Islamic Holy War and the Fate of Non-Muslims* (Amherst, NY: Prometheus, 2005).

12. Surah 90:12–13.

13. *Surah* 24.33.

14. Sahih Muslim Book 010, Hadith number 3901. For an online version of this and other hadiths, see http://hadithcollection.com.

15. See Rizwi Faizer, ed., *The Life of Muhammad: Al-Waqidi's Kitab al-Maghazi*, trans. Amal Ismail and Abdul Kader Tayob (Milton Park, NY: Routledge, 2011); Ma'mar ibn Rashid, *The Expeditons: An Early Biography of Muhammad*, ed. and trans. Sean W. Anthony (New York: New York University Press, 2014). This last biography is available at Internet Archive, https://archive.org/details/TheExpeditions.

16. Sayyid Abul A'la Mawdudi, *Tafhim al-Qur'an—The Meaning of the Quran*, vol. 1 (Lahore: Islamic Books, 1976), 329, Internet Archive, https://archive.org/stream/Maududi-Tafhim-al-Quran-The_Meaning_of_the_Quran/004%20-%20An-Nisa%20%28%20The%20Women%20%29#page/n15.

17. Sayyid Qutb, *In the Shade of the Qur'an*, trans. Adil Salahi, vol. 3, Surah 4 (Leicester: Islamic Foundation, 2015), 112–15.

18. Qutb, *Shade*, 114.

19. Qutb, *Shade*, 111–15. A complete set of his commentaries and some other key writtings are at Internet Archive, https://archive.org/details/texts?and%5B%5D=Sayyid+Qutb+&sin=.

20. Mohamed Mahmoud, "To Beat or Not to Beat: On the Exegetical Dilemmas over Qur'ān 4:34," *Journal of the American Oriental Society* 126.4 (October–December 2006), 537–50.

21. This Hadith is found in *Sahih Bukhari*, vol. 001, book 006, Hadith number 301, which is generally regarded as a very reliable source.

22. Surah 48:29.

23. Surah 98:6.

24. Matthew 5:44.

25. Ronald Segal, *Islam's Black Slaves* (New York: Farrar, Straus & Giroux, 2001); *Guardian*, July 18, 2018, www.theguardian.com/world/2018/jul/19/us-modern-slavery-report-global-slavery-index.

26. Lizzie Dearden, "Grooming Gangs Abused More Than 700 Women and Girls around Newcastle after Police Appeared to Punish Victims," *The Independent*, February 23, 2018, www.independent.co.uk/news/uk/crime/grooming-gangs-uk-britain-newcastle-serious-case-review-operation-sanctuary-shelter-muslim-asian-a8225106.html.

27. Bernard Smith, "'They Sell Africans Over There': Libya's Slave Trade," *Al Jazeera*, November 28, 2017, www.aljazeera.com/news/2017/11/they-sell-africans-there-libyas-slave-trade-171128142327034.html.

Conclusion

1. Matthew 28:19.

2. Matthew 24:14, cf. Acts 1:1–8.

3. Edward Conze, *Buddhism: Its Essence and Development* (Oxford: Bruno Cassirer, 1957), 18.

4. Nirad C. Chaudhuri, *Hinduism: A Religion to Live By* (Oxford: Oxford India, 1997), 294.

5. Chaudhuri, *Hinduism*, 316–29.

6. Chaudhuri, *Hinduism*, 294–99.

7. Chaudhuri, *Hinduism*, 299.

8. Kenneth Ingham, *Reformers in India, 1793–1883: An Account of the Work of Christian Missionaries on Behalf of Social Reform* (New York: Octagon, 1973).

9. Chaudhuri, *Hinduism*; Paul Williams, *The Unexpected Way: On Converting from Buddhism to Catholicism* (Edinburgh: T&T Clark, 2002).

10. P. Crone and M. Cook, *Hagarism: The Making of the Islamic World* (Cambridge: Cambridge University Press, 1977).

11. Jacob Neusner, *A Rabbi Talks with Jesus* (Montreal and Kingston: McGill-Queen's University Press, 2001).

12. Although it is hard to find published sources on this in English, one can find numerous references on Islamic websites, e.g., Al-Islam.org, www.al-islam.org/articles/beliefs-why-follow-family-prophet-s.

13. Gavin Flood, *An Introduction to Hinduism* (Cambridge: Cambridge University Press, 2005), 12.

14. Matthew 24.

15. Begin with the later works of sociologist Rodney Stark, beginning with his groundbreaking book *The Rise of Christianity: How the Obscure, Marginal Jesus Movement Became the Dominant Religious Force in the Western World in a Few Centuries* (San Francisco: Harper, 1997), and his *For the Glory of God: How Monotheism Led to Reformations, Science, Witch-hunts, and the End of Slavery* (Princeton, NJ: Princeton University Press, 2003). Other valuable works are Zondervan's books on church history and other important topics, e.g., Everett Ferguson, *Church History, Volume One: From Christ to the Pre-Reformation* (Grand Rapids: Zondervan, 2013); John D. Woodbridge and Frank A. James, *Church History, Volume Two: From Pre-Reformation to the Present Day* (Grand Rapids: Zondervan, 2013).

16. Luke 1:1–4.

17. Stark, *Glory of God*, 291–365.

18. Kevin Belmonte, *William Wilberforce* (Grand Rapids: Zondervan, 2007).

19. Matthew 5:16.

Scripture Index

Subject Index

Author Index